# The
# Mysteries
# in
# Your Life

REV. M. RAYMOND, o.c.s.o.

MILWAUKEE • THE BRUCE PUBLISHING COMPANY

NIHIL OBSTAT:

 Fr. M. Charles English, o.c.s.o.
 Fr. M. Benjamin Clark, o.c.s.o.
 *Censores Ordinis*

IMPRIMI POTEST:

 ✠ Most Rev. M. Ignace Gillet, o.c.s.o.
 *Abbas Generalis*

NIHIL OBSTAT:

 John A. Schulien, s.t.d.
 *Censor Librorum*

IMPRIMATUR:

 ✠ William E. Cousins
 *Archbishop of Milwaukee*

March 8, 1965

*Library of Congress Catalog Card Number: 65–20547*

To
MARY IMMACULATE — OUR MOTHER
whose life was
ONE LONG MYSTERY
from
THE ANNUNCIATION on to THE ASSUMPTION
and to her beloveds:

THE LOUIS JACOBS FAMILY
which, by another great mystery of God's love,
has grown to include
Three Little Flanagans
PATRICIA, MARY MARGARET, and CHRISTINE,
this little effort is lovingly dedicated.

# Other Works by Father Raymond

## BOOKS

THE MAN WHO GOT EVEN WITH GOD
THREE RELIGIOUS REBELS
THE FAMILY THAT OVERTOOK CHRIST
BURNT OUT INCENSE
GOD GOES TO MURDERERS' ROW
LOVE DOES SUCH THINGS
A NEW WAY OF THE CROSS
GOD, A WOMAN, AND THE WAY
THESE WOMEN WALKED WITH GOD
THE LESS TRAVELLED ROAD
YOU
THE TRAPPISTS, THE REDS, AND YOU
THIS IS YOUR TOMORROW . . . AND TODAY
NOW!
YOUR HOUR
THIS IS LOVE

## BOOKLETS

*Is Your Home Like This?*
*Life Is Someone!*
*The God-Man's Double*
*You Are Leading a Dangerous Life*
*Are You?*
*Say "Fiat" and Remake Your World*
*Life Is a Divine Romance*
*You Can Set the World on Fire!*
*What Are You Doing to Jesus Christ?*
*Have You Met God?*
*What's Wrong? (College Graduates)*
*Doubling for the Mother of God*
*Whispers From the Wings*
*Running Off With God*
*Do You Want Life and Love?*
*Help God Be a Success*
*A Trappist Does a Startling Thing for You*
*For Your Own Defense*
*A Message From Those Killed in Action*
*A Letter to Mothers Whose Sons Are in the Service*
*Facts About Reason, Revelation and Religion*

# Contents

# THE MYSTERIES IN YOUR LIFE

## CHAPTER ONE

## Facts

~~~~~~~~~~~~~~~~~~~~~~~~~~~~~~~~~~~~~~~~~~

IN MYSTERY you "live and move and have your being."

Deny that and you are admitting that you have never truly lived.

Just look about you: at this very moment there stand in our land tall bins filled with wheat — the surplus of those seasons which yielded bumper crops; yet, in other lands, millions of our fellow humans have not enough bread. Tonight more than half the human race will go to bed hungry; yet, more than likely, this very day saw tons of potential bread poured into elevators for storage.

Those few facts place palpable mystery before us, especially when we are so persistent in the proclamation of our basic dogma that "all men have been created equal."

Then again, consider drink: practically everyone will subscribe to Scripture's testimony that God gave wine "to cheer the heart of man"; yet who can count the human hearts that are aching and even breaking this very day because of alcoholism? Is that not mysterious?

Next, how proud we are to hold that among the God-given, unalienable rights, which every man enjoys, the first is the right to life. Yet, while medical men wondrously prolong human life, countless wedded couples are bent on preventing it. Worse still, there are those who will take life away from the unborn. It is estimated that, annually, there are at least a million abortions in these United States; yet we go on claiming that we love life, and that even the unborn infant has an unalienable right to it.

Take the family: we insist — and rightly — that it is the very

1

basis of the State, and that the home is the backbone of society. How mystifying it is, then, to find one out of every three marriages ending in the divorce courts, and the home becoming more and more, for far too many, just a street address and a letter-drop.

These are facts; undeniable facts. Will you deny that they present you with mystery? Look at some more: Present-day man prides himself on his high degree of civilization. Yet, when did savagery and barbarity more abound? Never was a generation entertained as is the present one; yet boredom is almost universal. More and more leisure is being sought; more and more of it is being found; yet, more and more of it is being squandered in feverish, and often futile, activity. Today pleasure is had for the asking; yet, when was there such discontent? Throughout the world peoples are crying as did the people of old, "Peace, Peace — and there is no peace." Talk about living amid mysteries!

Now look within yourself. How is it that you have such high aspirations, yet so few realizations of them? How is it that you, and I, and just about every other man and woman, who so earnestly long to be noble, large-hearted, generous, truly kind, so often find ourselves ignoble, petty, shrivelled-souled, and down-right mean? How is it that we who again and again resolve to be honest, upright, integral, and true so often find ourselves deceitful, dishonest, and basely untrue? How is it that we can have such lofty ideals about being chivalrous toward God and man, knightly in our purity and love, yet, in real life and actual living, find ourselves writhing with lusts?

As Chesterton put it years ago: "Whatever else men have believed, they have always believed that there was something wrong with man" (*Everlasting Man,* p. 60).

Ovid, that ancient pagan, recognized this mystery within himself, and expressed it: "I see clearly the better thing, and I approve of it heartily; yet it is the despicable thing that I do." Who cannot echo him? Even the mighty St. Paul paraphrased this pagan, and did so while under Divine Inspiration. In lines each of us can apply to ourselves Paul confessed: "I do not understand what I do, for what I wish, I do not; what I hate, I do." He gave partial explanation of this mystifying contradiction found universally in man when he wrote: "My inner self agrees joyfully with the Law of God, but I see another law in my bodily members warring against the Law which my mind approves" (Rom 7:15 sqq.).

While that explains the contradiction between his deeds and his desires, it does not explain the mystery in his makeup which brings this contradiction into being. Why this war within Paul? Why the same war within you, me, every man?

Hamlet could exclaim: "What a piece of work is a man! How noble in reason! how infinite in faculty! in form, in moving, how express and admirable! in action how like an angel! in apprehension how like a god! . . . And yet, to me, what is this quintessence of dust?" Pascal declared: "What a monster is man . . . the repository of truth, a sink of doubt and error; the glory and scum of the universe" (*Pensées,* 434). St. Augustine wrote in his *City of God:* "Man is a wonderful being, because God made him in His own image, yet he remains a mystery to himself."

You are a mystery — even to yourself. So let us look into these mysteries in your life and try to find a solution.

Practically all good mystery stories open with the finding of a corpse. The mystery story of your life opens with the finding of more than one corpse. Here are the facts:

At the opening of your story there are found the dead bodies of two men, whom you must recognize as the bodies of your brothers. Each has been murdered. In connection with each murder there was an altar. That acceptable sacrifice had been offered to God on each of these altars is among the fundamental reasons for each murder. Hence, it is obvious that the fratricides take on the nature of sacrilege.

But the fact of all facts is that you were involved in each slaying!

Of course you will deny all complicity, indignantly assert your innocence, and demand that the charge of fratricide leveled against you be dismissed as utterly outrageous. But we are dealing with known facts. These victims were your brothers. You are deeply involved in their deaths. Yet, calm yourself; for these are not recent murders, nor are you now being apprehended to be brought to trial. These cases were solved in the long, long ago; for the first slaying took place in what can be called the beginning of time for the human race; while the second occurred in what is known as the fullness of time. But if you would solve the mysteries in your own life today, and the many mysteries you will face in the future, you will be wise to unravel once again the mysteries that surround the death of Abel and the death of Jesus Christ.

In the deaths of these two lie the secrets to your life. Find out why they were murdered and you have found the solution to *everything* that bewilders you in the world without, and *everything* that puzzles you and perplexes you in the world within.

Sophisticated science may not be one bit interested in these two corpses, but that is only because such science is not truly wise. Real science leads to wisdom; and wisdom is what we need for proper living. So it will be to Theology, the Science of all sciences, that we will have recourse in order to solve the mysteries of your life and thus enable you to live wisely.

That is not meant to disparage in any least way the mighty sciences of our day, but simply to point beyond them and indicate their ultimate purpose and their real perfection. Because man is not a machine, we must call upon more than the physical sciences to tell us who man is, whence he came, why he is here, and where he is headed.

Appreciate science and admire scientists we must. But, despite their stupendous capabilities and near-miraculous achievements, life — and death — still remain mysteries to these men. What is more, we have to face the fact that science has not only produced awe and admiration; it has also generated anguish, anxiety, bewilderment, and fear.

In splitting the atom, science has split the world. So true is that that many of your thoughtful contemporaries are pondering at great length those lines in St. Peter's second Epistle which tell that "the day of the Lord will come as a thief. Then the heavens will pass away in a roaring flame and its elements will burn up and be dissolved" (2 Pt 3:10). Many suspect that "thief" is already on his way; for they are fully and frightfully aware of the possibility that, today, a man can press a button in a room thousands of miles away and, out of that space beyond earth's atmosphere, an orbiting satellite will drop a bomb which will zero down on and obliterate the city in which they live and blight an enormous area surrounding it. Small wonder some are speaking of "the divinity of the bomb" which they know is "brooding over your world."

Even sober theologians add their voices to these dire predictions. Paul Tillich, the highly respected Protestant theologian, has claimed that the words "laying the foundations of the earth," met with so often in both Testaments, really mean: "binding their forces." He explains by saying that so long as the unruly powers of the smallest part of our material world were restrained by cohesive structures, a place was provided in which life could grow, history develop, words be heard, truth discovered, and the Eternal One adored. "But," he adds, "out of the fertile soil of the earth a being was generated and nourished who was able to find the key to the foundations of all beings. That being was man. He has discovered the key which can unlock the forces of the ground, those forces which were bound when the foundations of the earth were laid. He has begun to use that key. He has subjected the basis of life and thought and will to *his* will. And he has willed destruction." Challenge his exegesis you may; but can anyone deny his conclusion?

Science and technology have scored such successes that the human intellect staggers. The minute but might-laden atom as well as the measureless stretches of outer space seem to lie in the hands of puny man, and we have reason to fear, for, with chilling clarity we see that the very things man has conquered may yet conquer man.

A more subtle, but nonetheless real, destruction is going on all about you because of these same two factors: technology and science. In the world of work, the machine, which first depersonalized man, is now supplanting him. In more than one field IBM's have already taken the place of the human individual, and promise to take his place in many more fields shortly. Technology, with ever increasing speed, conditions man and is steadily controlling him. Radio, television, instant news service, entertainment, education are homogenizing the masses to such an extent that it is rare today to find an individual who does not feel helpless, futile, and lonely — an isolated nonentity who is readily expendible. Science, supplanting Faith in the minds of many, is destroying the basis of man's true nobility.

In the not too distant past most people believed they were children of God, possessed of an immortal soul, and, hence, destined for an eternal existence. They also considered themselves endowed with a faculty which made them self-determining, and, hence, fully responsible persons. Today, more and more doubt that they were made by God, are endowed with immortality, gifted with free will, and graced with a spiritual intellect which differentiates them essentially from those animals who are so easily conditioned to react to definite stimuli. Roots have been cut and contact lost with the very source of man's true being.

Our world is working feverishly at the experiment of forming a civilized but non-Christian mentality. It may be somewhat reassuring to hear a man of T. S. Eliot's penetration say that the experiment is bound to fail and to urge us, while awaiting its collapse, to "redeem the time" so that Faith may be preserved alive for the dark ages which lie ahead. But it may well be asked where is one to find the fortitude required to await the collapse, or the fire to keep the flame of Faith alive in a world growing so cold and dark? I believe the answer is to be discovered only by those who will look at the two corpses found in the opening of your story and see how deeply involved they are in those two murders.

John Henry Cardinal Newman almost a hundred years before the Age of the Atom, the Age of the Jet, the Age of Outer Space, the Age of Anxiety, the Age of Fear, and this dark and ever darkening Age of Unreason, wrote: "Were it not for this voice, speaking so clearly in my conscience and my heart, I should be an atheist, or a pantheist, or a polytheist when I looked into the world. To consider the world in its length and breadth, its various history, the many races of men, their starts, their fortunes, their mutual alienation, their conflicts; their enterprises, their aimless courses, their random achievements and acquirement . . . the greatness and littleness of man, his far-reaching aims, his short duration, the curtain hung over his futurity, the disappointments of life, the defeat of good, the success of evil, physical pain, mental anguish, the prevalence and intensity of sin . . . that condition of the whole race, so fearfully yet exactly described in the Apostle's words, *'having no hope and without God in the world'* — all this is a vision to dizzy and appal; and inflicts upon the mind the sense of a profound mystery, which is absolutely beyond human solution."

Newman agrees that "in mystery you live and move and have your being." Newman disagrees seemingly with the fact that we are going to find a solution; but it is only seeming — for the solution we find is one that is not beyond human reason, when that reason is aided by grace and God.

But, as do we, Newman insists that we are facing facts. He exclaims: "What shall be said to this heart-piercing, reason-bewildering *fact?* I can only answer, that either there is no Creator, or this living society of men is in a true sense discarded from His presence. . . . And so I argue about the world; if there be a God, *since* there is a God, the human race is implicated in some terrible aboriginal calamity. It is out of joint with the purposes of its Creator. This is a fact, a fact as true as the fact of its existence . . ." (*Apologia pro Vita Sua,* pp. 241–243).

The Cardinal finally concluded that the explanation of these facts lay precisely where we will find it — in the explanation of what brought on the slaughter of the two victims we have found at the opening of the mystery story that is your life. He stated his conclusion in this fashion: ". . . thus the doctrine of what is theologically called original sin becomes to me almost as certain as that the world exists, and as the existence of God."

That is the truth that will break upon the mind of any thinker if he will regard closely these two corpses. One is the corpse of the first man ever to know death. The other is the Corpse of the only Man ever to overcome death. That our world has not looked at these corpses thoughtfully enough to unravel the mysteries bound

up in these murders is one of the basic reasons for the fear-filled
and fear-filling condition of our present-day world. Sin lies at the
bottom of both of these deaths — and our world is fast losing, if
it has not already lost, its sense of sin. But to lose that sense is to
lose touch with all that makes life worth living; for it is to lose
contact with the only realities that ennoble man: Divinity, humanity, liberty, responsibility, and the potentiality of acquiring eternal
reward.

Far from saying too much, that hardly says enough; for sin
connotes God. Strictly speaking, we cannot sin against anyone
but God. Lose our sense of sin, and we have lost our sense of
God. Lose our sense of sin and God, and we have lost our sense
of man. For it is only man who can sin. Paradoxical as it may
sound, it can be said that in your ability to sin and thus offend
God lies the essence of your nobility and of your likeness to God;
for the power to sin lies in your free will. It is your liberty that
marks you out as close kin to Divinity. As Chesterton remarked:
"If a man could not be bad he could never be good."

The corpse of the first man ever murdered tells you much about
yourself. But it is not the murder of Abel itself that will do the
explaining. It is what lies behind that murder. Not Cain's hate.
Not Cain's jealousy. Not Cain's death-breeding selfishness. But
the legacy Cain inherited from his parents. Adam and Eve, however, were also your parents — your first parents. So your involve-
ment in this first of all human crimes is real because of that
relationship.

Do not think you are being asked to look upon too distant a
deed. The veritable chaos of contemporary society derives from
the identical source which produced this first murder. Original sin,
mentioned by Newman, is not only an evil fact of the past; it is
the fountainhead of every present-day evil. The legacy left to
every descendant of Adam and Eve is the same: that inclination
to evil. "Man," wrote Pascal, "is more unintelligible without this
mystery [of original sin] than this mystery is unintelligible to man"
(*Pensées*, 434).

The key to the murder of Abel gives you the key to every other murder — even to those headlining this morning's paper. And the senseless defense offered by the first murderer is the same: *"Am I my brother's keeper?"*

You most certainly are! As is every president, premier, prime minister, and member of Polituburo. But before you or they can ever become your brother's keeper, you and they must learn how to become your own keeper. That neither you nor they will ever learn unless you look deep into the mystery that surrounds the second Corpse. Sin, again, is the key. But, this time, it is not only the original sin of your first parents. In this second crime you are more personally involved. So am I. The Corpse of Christ will explain the mysteries of your life and mine; for no one of us is really living unless we are fully *"alive to God in Christ Jesus"* (Rom 6:11). Hence, if you are ever to unravel the mysteries in your life — and they are multiple — or if you are ever to acquire real understanding of the mystery of your life, you must hear the indefatigable St. Paul proclaiming "without stint the mystery hidden for ages and generations — *Christ in you,* your hope of glory" (Col 1:26, 27). If you listen to his hymn of joy, his lyrical outburst of gratitude, you will never be afraid. Paul bares his soul, and unburdens yours and mine as he says "Blessed be the Father of our Lord Jesus Christ, who *in Christ* has blessed us with every manner of spiritual blessing. . . . These blessings correspond to his choice of us *in Christ* before the foundation of the world. . . . Out of love he predestined us for himself to become *through Jesus Christ* his adopted children. . . . With this grace he has inundated us, by imparting to us all manner of wisdom and practical knowledge, making known to us the mystery of his will . . . namely, to gather all creation both in heaven and on earth under one head, *Christ"* (Eph 1:3–10).

In those words is more mystery. But in them is also the solution to all the mysteries of your life. For that is the love song of your soul as well as the love song of the heart of God. It tells you, as first fact, that you are older than your years and younger than the day of your birth; for it gives you the key to the mystery of your being even as it points to the glorious destiny that is your end.

Catch all that is implied in that phrase "before the foundation of the world," and you can give proper reply, one deep with the depths of God, to the simple-sounding question: "How old are you" — or — "When were you born?" For the fact that you were chosen out *"in Christ* — before the foundation of the world" — gives you the lead you need to unravel the mystery that is you.

# CHAPTER TWO

## First Mystery . . . Your Exact Age

~~~~~~~~~~~~~~~~~~~~~~~~~~~~~~~~~~~~~~~~~~~~~~~~~~~~~~

*"Before the Foundation of the World . . . You Were."*

"How old are you?" sounds like a very simple question, one that surely can be answered with ease. Were you asked that today, undoubtedly your reply would be ready. Some can give, not only the day of the week, the month of the year, and the hour of the day, but even the precise minute of the hour. But such an exact reply barely scratches the surface of the question; it comes nowhere near its heart. For whenever a human asks this simple-sounding question, overtones and undertones that tell of the Eternal and the Divine are set vibrating for those who seek adequate answers that bespeak the ultimate. For, absolutely speaking, the simple question: "When were you born?" involves that dark, deep, Divine mystery called predestination. In other words, God had a reason, a Divinely deep reason, for bringing you to birth at the specific moment that He did. At that split-second in time, a Divine decree drawn up from all Eternity, which had to do with you, was fulfilled. That particular decree bespeaks a definite relation to God's overall Eternal Plan for the race of men and for His universe. You were wanted by God at that one moment. So the simple-sounding question: *"When* were you born?" is not so simple. It takes you into the Omniscience, the Omnipotence, and the Infinite Wisdom who is God.

Any question relating to your birth teems with mysteries; for each of them will demand replies whose roots are in Divine Wisdom. For instance: Why were you born of your particular parents, with all that meant for you in the way of physical and spiritual heredity — your nationality and temperament; with all that meant to you in the way of environment, social standing, upbringing and education? Why were you born in your particular village, town, or city; in that particular state or country? There was a specific reason for each of these specified realities. It was a God-conceived and eternally-decreed reason. It was a reason sired by Infinite Wisdom and prompted by Infinite Goodness. It had to do with your particular mission in life. It was, and is, connected with God's ultimate Glory and humankind's eternal state.

It is not often that we dwell thus on our births. But the truth is that you could not be you, nor could I be I, had not God chosen our particular parents for each of us. They were like so much carefully selected clay with which He would model and mold to His Infinite desire and for His infinitely wise purpose the specific individuals He had in His Mind and Heart before He called forth the daystar. Our particular parents were the only ones in His almost limitless creation who could furnish the elements He required for the makeup He had determined would be yours and mine.

It is well to get our particular parents in focus. It is rewarding to realize that they were the flint, the only flint in His far-flung universe, from which He could strike the specific spark He wanted to be you — and the one He wanted to be me. Our parents were not merely parts of God's plan for us; they were His partners in the execution of His Eternal Decree concerning us. Looking at this truth gives us more than respect and reverence for our parents; it gives us more than love. It gives us something that borders on adoration — for they were so close to God in bringing us into being. They were essential to the many mysteries contained in the one mystery we call our birth.

Why you were born just *when* you were born; why you were born just *where* you were born; why you were born *of whom* you were born are questions that have one explicit answer: God's Will, or, better still, God's Wisdom. The infinitely wise God could find no better way to have His purpose attained than by giving you your particular parents, and having them bring you forth at a certain time and at a certain place. In other words, under God's hands, they gave you exactly what you needed so that you could discharge the unique mission God had decreed should be yours. Doubt that, and you are questioning both Omniscience and Omnipotence. The unchallengeable truth is that God fitted you perfectly for the task that is to be yours in time. You are not only an apt instrument for His work, you are a perfectly adjusted instrument; for God never makes a mistake. "All His works are without repentance," and you are one of His greatest works.

All that is true of you no matter where you were born: in house, hovel, or hospital; in castle or cattle shed. All that is true of you whether your parents were legitimately married or illegitimately mated. Humans are needed before a human can be born; but human birth, like human conception, is a work of God. St. Paul's words still ring true: you were "chosen out in Christ before the foundations of the world" and you have been "predestined" by God "to become through Jesus Christ his adopted child." It is necessary to leave the realm of the purely human and temporal and enter that of the Eternal and Divine, if you are to give adequate answer to the simple-sounding question: "How old are you?"

Sister Madeleva, C.S.C., once answered this question in a line of poetry:

Older am I than any star.

That may seem like no reply at all. Yet it is the only exact reply about her own age as well as yours. For if the question is rephrased to read: "When did you first begin to be?" or "Precisely when did you come into being?" you must reply as Wisdom does in the Book of Proverbs and say: "The Lord made me his when first he began his work, at the birth of time, before his creation began. Long, long ago, before earth was fashioned, I held my course. Already I lay in the womb, when the depths were not yet in being, when no springs of water had yet broken; when I was born, the mountains had not yet sunk on their firm foundations, and there were no hills; not yet had he made the earth, or the rivers, or the solid framework of the world. I was there when he built the heavens, when he fenced in the waters with a vault inviolable, when he fixed the sky overhead, and levelled the fountain-springs of the deep. I was there when he enclosed the sea within its confines, forbidding the waters to transgress their assigned limits, when he poised the foundations of the world" (Prv 8.22 sq.).

Therefore . . . "Say farewell to your childishness, and learn to live" (Prv 9:6). For it is indisputably true that ". . . as days are told the earth is younger than you are old," for before God said: "Let there be light . . ." you had existence in His Mind and Will. The timeless Maker of time had you as a thought before time began. The sole Sovereign of being had decreed you were to be before He created Adam and Eve. From eternity you came. To eternity you go. In the eternal you have ever been. And this basic mystery about you, which lies in eternity, will tell you much about the many mysteries you face in time; for each of those has something to do with the fundamental and final purpose God had in mind when from among limitless possible beings He selected you to be. That selection was as deliberate, and as purposeful, in its degree, as was the Divine determination to send His only Son into the world that the world of men might become His sons.

Jean-Paul Sartre may seem like a strange witness to call forth, but he does bear out the contention we are making about the only adequate answer to the human is the Divine. When he contemplated the mystery of man he wrote: ". . . God is first of all apprehended by the 'heart' of man as the being who proclaims man's existence and defines him in relation to his ultimate and fundamental project. . . . God, the supreme value and end in the transcendental order, represents the permanent and ultimate limit of being in terms of which man insists upon being told what he himself is. To be a man is to move toward the attainment of the existence of God. Or, in other words, man is fundamentally a desire to be God."

That is not blasphemy. That is not even new. Many, many centuries before Sartre's time, Origen had written: "It is man's duty to achieve this likeness [to God] by striving to imitate God so that, having originally acquired, through being honored by his creation in God's image, the possibility of attaining perfection, he may finally achieve a perfect likeness [to God] by performing his allotted tasks."

That is why you were born. That is why you were brought into this world. That is why you were brought forth at that time and place, and of those parents God had required to fulfill his all-wise plan for you. You were made to the image and likeness of God. You were made to know Him, love Him, serve Him, as any catechism will tell you. But to know and love God is to become "like unto God." You can do that, and do it perfectly only one way — "in Him, through Him, and with Him," who named Himself the Way — *Jesus Christ.*

Consequently Sartre, Origen, and the catechism are saying the same thing in different words; but they all sublimate to the one fact: you were made to be *Christ.*

That is meant to shock. We are dealing with mysteries. Before we can solve them we have to be shocked. St. Paul told you that you have been "predestined." That was his word. It denotes an eternal, irrevocable decree on the part of God, which was in reality an explosion of infinite love that was to be followed by an almost eternal "fallout" of loving mercy and merciful love. Predestination means that from all eternity God had determined that He would one day bring you forth as a mirror of His own majesty, as a creature who would contain within yourself a miniature of His mighty universe, a microcosm that would be His very own image and likeness.

Predestination means that God, with Wisdom which is unerring, selected the uniqueness that you would need to be what He wanted you to be. Nothing whatsoever was left to chance. He fitted you perfectly for the one role He would have you play; fitted you down to the color of your hair and eyes and skin, the shape of your face and its every feature. He predetermined, before time was, just what talents He would give you, and which you were to at least double; what tendencies to evil He would permit in your makeup. And this decree of predestination left you with a liberty as wide, in its way, as the very liberty of the infinitely free God. What a mystery that is: absoluteness on the part of God down to the number of the hairs of your head, yet such utter liberty on your part, His creature, as to enable you to become either like Cain or like Christ!

That is the depth of the mystery of your birth. God foresaw what your first parents would do. He saw Eve disobeying before Eve was. He heard the cry of Abel's blood before Abel was conceived. Yet, in His love, He predestined you to be descendant of Adam and Eve, kin to these eldest of your brothers, Abel and Cain, but also kin to that "first-born of many brethren," Jesus Christ, and through Him to become a child of God. Paul tells how you were predestined by God "to become through Jesus Christ his adopted child." Paul draws the consequences from such a fact when he tells you that "You have not received a spirit of bondage so that you are again in fear, but you have received a spirit of adoption as sons, in virtue of which we cry: 'Abba! Father!' The Spirit himself joins his testimony to that of our spirit that we are children of God. But if we are children, we are heirs also: heirs indeed of God and joint heirs with Christ . . ." (Rom 8:15–17).

God chose you to be heir to His Kingdom. From all eternity God decreed that you should be His legatee. By an irrevocable determination He predestined you to be kin to His only Son, and consequently "joint heir" with Him who properly speaking was to be, and is, the only Heir.

Pondering this mystery called predestination you will come to see how futile, foolish, and even bordering on the blasphemous it is to grow angry, as so many humans do, with the endownment that is theirs from an all-wise God.

What would you think of a violet if, knowing that it could glorify God only by being a violet, and that if it fulfilled its function it would know everlastingness and bliss, it nevertheless longed to be a lily? Stupidity could not be more stupid, could it? Yet we humans who know that God has predestined us, and know something of what predestination means, how often in fact do we not do what the imagined violet never did: we envy the lily! What set Cain to the slaughter of his brother? What killed Christ? When will we manifest intelligence enough to accept ourselves as God made us and rejoice to be just as He has willed us to be — with these many limitations and these few assets? When will we glory in the mystery of His decrees of predestination knowing that we could not be more wisely shaped or fashioned, more liberally endowed for the work that is ours, more fully equipped to become what God wants us to become — Christ, and joint heirs with Christ?

Pondering rightly on predestination would not only end fear, anxiety, frustration; not only smother all envy, jealousy, and unrest; but generate joy. Ponder rightly on the many mysteries in your birth and you will feel only gratitude to the God who predestined you.

The key to both of these mysteries is given by St. Paul in these words: *"Out of love* he predestined us for himself" (Eph 1:5). The mystery of your birth, of your life, and all your living, as the mystery of creation itself, is the mystery of love. "God is love," said St. John, then went on to ink in God's blueprint for you and me and every human by adding: "God's love was made manifest among us by the fact that God sent his only-begotten Son into the world that we might have life through him" (1 Jn 4:8, 9).

John's words are substantiated by those of the Word Himself. For Christ said: "I am life" (Jn 14:6). He even specified His mission to earth by saying: "I have come that they may have life and have it in abundance" (Jn 10:10).

You were predestined to have life; you were to have human life; more, you were to have divine-human life; you were to have eternal life with God the Father, God the Son, and God the Holy Spirit. You were to have all this life because God is Love; you were to live a life of love. That is what "predestination" ultimately means for you personally.

Follow the steps closely, and you will never again go astray. God the Father, by way of eternal generation, communicates divine life to the Word. That Word becomes Man. "Just as the Father has life in himself, so did he give it to the Son to have life in himself." But the Son would not keep that life to Himself. He said so explicitly: He came to communicate that life to us men. Not mere human life — which we already had; but that divine life which the Word had from Eternity. He would pour that life out on men through the humanity He had assumed. But, in creating us, God made us free. Hence, that divine life, which the Son was so anxious to communicate that He willingly died to do so, must be received by us . . . by lively Faith, and through the Sacraments. "To as many as welcomed him he gave the power to become children of God . . . of his fullness we have all received" (Jn 1:12–16).

Thus Christ is the Center of the Divine Plan — for you and me and all mankind, Paul tells us, and for all creation. One Greek text reads: "It is God's will to make Christ the chief, the head of all creation." The mystery of your life, and all the mysteries in your living, then, center on Jesus Christ — and this by an eternal decree of predestination made by Him who is Love.

Love brought you into being. Love gave you life and your uniqueness. Love gave you a share in His own divine life. Love, therefore, gave you love. That is evident if you look into your being; for what are you but a steadily pulsing craving to give love and to receive love? That longing is satisfied fully, in both its craving to give and its craving to receive, only by your being "in Christ Jesus." St. Paul has summed up this truth in a few thought-filled and thought-filling lines: "Therefore, follow God's example, as his very dear children, and let your conduct be guided by love, as Christ also loved us and delivered himself for us as an offering to God, a sacrifice that has an agreeable fragrance" (Eph 5:1, 2). There are your lifelines which were drawn for you from before the beginning of time!

The experienced psychiatrist can look deep into the subconscious and the unconscious and see there things the patient never dreamed existed. These men probe wisely and well. It is prudent on their part to look into sibling rivalries within your family. But it would be the height of wisdom and prudence to go back to the first sibling rivalry we have record of, and learn from Cain and Abel much that affects their patients of the present day. Let them gaze on Eve holding the body of Abel. It may lead them to the discovery of the "primary" in many of the cases they have to handle. It would solve many of the mysteries they now cannot solve.

# CHAPTER THREE

# This Mystery Brings Brightness Into Your Life

*The* Pietà *Michelangelo Never Sculptured and*
*The* Annunciation *Gabriel Never Made*

FEW of the works of the great Michelangelo have moved as many, or have moved as deeply, as has his justly famed scultpure known as the *Pietà*.

In Italian the word means "pity." And pity arises spontaneously in the human heart once that sculpture is glimpsed; pity for the Mother who holds the Corpse of her only Son — God's only Son, too — on her lap. Pity, also, for the Son of that grieving Mother.

When you gaze on this Mother and Son, you are looking upon the representation in stone of one of the deepest mysteries of God, and the mystery of all mysteries for man. For this is the Corpse of no mere man who has been done to death; nor is that any ordinary Mother who holds the lifeless Body of her Son upon her knees. You are gazing upon God as a Corpse. You are looking on the only truly Eternal and Immortal as dead in time. You are contemplating the utterly incomprehensible: Divinity, despite infinite impassibility, done to death — and a Virgin Mother holding on her lap, even as she once carried in her womb, *all men.*

Once you probe with your intellect on what lies beneath that which your senses reveal to you, you will want to change the Italian *Pietà* to the more telling Latin word *Pietas.* For you will realize how eloquent that Corpse is of the distance filial love can go: "He was obedient unto death — even to death on the cross," because such was His Father's will. But the sculpture can tell of more than the loyalty and love in the Heart of the Son; it can tell, also, of the loyalty and love in the heart of the Mother. For just as the Corpse of the Son tells how far His love for the Father took Him, so the fact that It lies across the knees of His Mother tells how far love for the Son took her.

Michelangelo has caught the poignancy of the mystery as Mary felt it on Calvary just after the Body of her Son had been taken down from the cross. But the mystery did not begin there. Nor was this lovely Mother, with the Corpse of her only Son on her lap, the world's first *Pietà* — or example of *Pietas,* or filial love. For that you will have to go back to the other corpse found at the opening of your mystery-filled life story, and in your imagination gaze upon the *Pietà* Michelangelo never sculptured — that of Eve holding the corpse of Abel.

Imagine, if you can, what went on in the mind and heart of Eve as she sat holding that dead body that dark evening of the day of the world's first fratricide.

She had faced the mystery of life with her first conception. She and Adam had not been born as other men and women after them would be. So, when Cain first stirred to life beneath her heart, what wonder must she have experienced! Then when she brought forth her firstborn, what awe must have filled her as she looked upon that tiny body, aglow with life, which had just issued from within her own body. He must have seemed so small to her, so helpless, so weak, yet so lovable. What did it all mean? She had known labor and pain. God had promised she would. But this joy! What did the pain and labor mean now? Here was her boy snuggling to her breast; his tiny heart beating above her own. He was alive! — But what was life?

But as Cain grew and Abel came, Eve, like so many of her children down to this day, must have grown used to living with this mystery of life. Yet, ever at the back of her consciousness must have been that nagging, gnawing question about that other mystery God had promised. "Of every tree in Paradise thou shalt eat. But of the tree of knowledge of good and evil, thou shalt not eat. For in what day soever thou shalt eat of it, thou shalt die the death" (Gn 2:16, 17). Eve had eaten of that tree. She was still alive. She was still giving life to others. What, then, was this thing called *death?*

Now, as she held the corpse of Abel, Eve saw that God was faithful to His promises. The cold, stiffening body told her what death could do. But nothing, and no one, save God Himself, could ever tell her what death was.

Pity for Eve? — Most assuredly! Not only because she was the world's first mother to hold the lifeless body of her child, but more especially because of the deeper mystery behind the first human death. That deeper mystery was not the envy, jealousy, and anger of Cain which had led him on to becoming the world's first murderer, but what lay beyond and behind that: her own first sin. Cain's hand had taken away Abel's life. But Eve knew that what had raised Cain's hand against Abel was her own feminine curiosity, vanity, and pride which had led her on to disobeying God.

Greek tragedy seems tame indeed in the face of these biblical truths. Hecuba with the corpse of Polydorus stirs pity, but never to the depths that are reached by one who really contemplates Eve as the world's first *Pietà*. Mystery lay in her arms. Death was something completely new in her experience. But in her soul sounded over and over again: "in what day soever *thou* shalt eat. . . ." She knew what she had done to Abel!

The Woman above all women blest, depicted in Michelangelo's *Pietà*, though the Mother of Sorrows, could never have known the particular sorrow that pierced Eve's heart. For, though Christ was done to death by sin, both He who died because of sin and she who suffered as the result of it were the only sinless humans ever to walk our earth. Hence, while Mary grieved, perhaps as no other mother ever had or ever will grieve, she knew that she herself had no part in the slaying of her Son.

These two corpses present you with the mystery of death and the mystery of sin. Those two mysteries will be in your life as long as you are on earth. Eve learned what Mary learned on Calvary in a different way: "the wages that sin gives is death . . ." (Rom 6:23).

But just as Mary had hope because of what her Son had so

often said concerning the "third day," so Eve had her own hope which she, too, hugged to her breaking heart. For Eve had heard the "Annunciation" that Gabriel never made — and this "Annunciation" is the first joyful mystery in your life — and in the life of every man.

We know that the moment in which the angel announced to Mary that she was to be the Mother of God is the midmost moment of all time, and his words were the seeding of true hope for mankind. No other moment, and no other message, held more meaning for man — or for God. Yet this Mystery of the Annunciation goes back beyond Mary and Joseph, beyond Nazareth; it goes back to Paradise, to Adam and Eve: it goes back to the beginning of time — and to God who was, is, and ever will be, *Love*.

It was back there in the Garden, just after the first human sin had been committed, that God uttered the words which set hope alive for humankind. He addressed Himself to Satan, but His words were weighty with meaning for you, for me, and for all mankind: "I will put enmities between thee and the woman, and thy seed and her seed; she shall crush thy head, and thou shalt lie in wait for her heel" (Gn 3:15).

That is much more than a condemnation and a curse. Lucifer, whose one sin had lit the eternal fires of Hell, was again being condemned and cursed by God; but, in that curse and condemnation, mankind, who had just sinned in that one sin of Adam, their moral head, was being told what shepherds were to be told long ages afterwards as they watched their flocks one wintry night outside Bethlehem: "Do not fear! Listen: I am bringing you good news of great joy" (Lk 2:10). Mankind was being told what Mary would later be told by Gabriel: "Do not tremble! You have found favor in the eyes of God!" (Lk 1:30.) Mankind was being told about Christ and Calvary; about Easter and Pentecost; about Heaven and Eternal Bliss. And all that just after mankind had first sinned! You were there — so was I — in our first parents. You and I were involved in the mystery of that first sin — just as you and I are now involved in the greater mystery of Salvation. For we are children of Adam and Eve and, "in Christ Jesus," have been chosen out from all eternity to become children of God. We have been predestined, as we have already seen. We, in short, are totally enmeshed in the mystery of God's love.

For what is this first "annunciation" but Love's earliest articulation of His love for us? The story of the mysteries in your life cannot begin with any more appropriate words than: "Once upon eternity God fell in love with you."

That is what the real Annunciation — the first Joyful Mystery of the rosary — says of you, and of me. But if we would comprehend the full meaning in this wondrous mystery we will not focus on Gabriel and Mary at Nazareth alone. We will go back to the "annunciation" Gabriel never made; we will go back to the *Pietà* Michelangelo never carved and look long upon Eve with the corpse of Abel on her lap. Then we can look ahead to that other mother holding the Corpse of Him of whom Abel, in his life, in his sacrifice, and in his death, was symbol.

The real Annunciation speaks of death as well as of life; and, ultimately, tells more of eternity than it does of time. For Christ was born to die — and rise again; and by that Death and Resurrection to win for you and me the possibility of everlastingness with God, as He won for us the possibility of spending all our days and all our nights "in Christ Jesus" so long as we are in time and thus "in Him live, and move, and have our being." Gabriel, without using the words, spoke of sin, of sacrifice for sin, of tragedy which would issue in triumph — just as God did in that first "annunciation" in Eden. All was contained in the name Gabriel told Mary she was to call her Son — *Jesus*.

As you know, that name means *Savior*. But it is well to ask yourself just what it was that Jesus saved you from. Not from *suffering*. You have suffered in your life; you will suffer more before your life ends. He did not save you from *sorrow*. You have already known sorrow in your life; you will know more as you go on living. Not from *sickness or death*. For "it is appointed for all men once to die." Then, from what did Jesus save you? From one thing, and from only one thing: from Hell.

Christ saved you from Hell — and for Heaven. Look at the corpse of Abel and realize that had Christ not become a Corpse, Abel could never have entered Heaven. Look at the Corpse of

Christ and realize, with a freshened realization, that you, once you had become a corpse, would have gone to Hell had not God Himself become Man so that He might become a Corpse. Yes, Satan would have held you, me, and every child of Adam and Eve, in his grip for all eternity, had there not been that "annunciation" in Eden — and that other Annunciation in Nazareth.

In Eden God had said: "I will put enmities between thee and the woman. . . ." That did not mean between Satan and the sin-stained Eve who was standing hard by. That meant between Satan and the sinless one who had not yet been conceived — Mary Immaculate. God had said: ". . . between thy seed and her seed." By that He did not mean between the devil and the children of Adam's wife. He meant between the devil and the only Son of Mary's womb. God had said: ". . . she shall crush thy head." He referred not to Mary, but to her seed: *Christ*.

Again you see that Christ is the center of the Mystery, and the center of your life which is so full of mysteries. This Mystery takes you back to Paradise lost, as it takes you back to that original sin and the first "annunciation" or promise of a Redeemer. It takes you ahead, too, to Paradise regained as it implies the *Pietà* on Calvary even as it announces the Madonna of Bethlehem, as it speaks to the Virgin at Nazareth.

The "annunciation" that God made should set you trying to measure the bewilderment of Heaven the day God gave birth to Hope for all humans. Gabriel, along with Michael, Raphael, and the loyal nine choirs of Heaven's host saw Lucifer fall like lightning. They witnessed the awful anger of God and watched in awe as the brightest of Heaven's bright spirits was hurled into Hell. In that terror-filled moment Heaven's loyal army learned something of the meaning of sin and the wrath of their God. Yet this same host of Heaven looked on after man's first sin and watched their God, who had brought the everlasting fires of Hell into being because of the one sin of the angels, turn now to Satan and, while cursing and condemning him anew, give humans, who had just sinned by their disobeying, the promise of salvation. That was the moment angels heard God giving birth to something that will never die so long as humans live on earth; they heard Him giving birth to *Hope.*

The meaning of this mystery is filled with paradox. The two mothers this mystery recalls tell you more about human nature than modern psychology will ever discover.

If you would know why it is that so many of your plans stay only in outline, so many dreams are unfulfilled, look at Eve and the body lying lifeless across her knees. You are weak. But if you would also know why it is that you, who are so weak, have such power-laden, nobility-filled, truly towering aspirations, such chivalrous ideals and ideas which you hope somehow, some time to bring to reality, look at Mary and at the dead Christ. These two mothers and their two sons can unravel much of the mystery that is you.

Have you not often been deeply distressed because you found that your noblest self could be base; that your heart, which would harbor only the purest of desires, would so often be filled with fiery lusts; that your mind, which would feed only on the loftiest of ideas, could toy with trifles? Why is it that you are such a bundle of contradictions? — Look at Mary. Look at Eve. These two women mothered you. You actually exist in two natures; not only in the lower and the higher, as they are so often called, but in a human nature and one that is partly divine. Hence the conflict; hence the contradictions.

You, who are sinful, must attain sanctity. With all your vanity, conceit, and pride, you must yet walk in humility. You, who almost instinctively covet, must grow ever more indifferent and detached. You, who find so many lusts in your life, must live a life of purest love. The opposites still multiply. For you, who often hold the seeds of murder in your heart because of anger must smother that anger and render all such seeds sterile. You who are ever inclined to be mentally, morally, and physically lazy, must become electric with energy and life in mind, will, and body. You, who can be so mean and envious, must rise to heights of magnanimity, genuinely admiring others and paying them honest tribute of praise. You whose soul so often seems to shrivel, whose heart inclines to be craven, and who can be a very petty person, must stand up as one incapable of an ignoble thought or an unworthy gesture, one who has a heart open to all the world.

Is there any hope that you will ever measure up to such demands? Any hope that you will resolve these paradoxes and cancel out these contradictions? There is limitless hope! Look at Abel. Look at Christ. Catch all the resonances in the mystery of the Annunciation, and you will come to know yourself — and your God, and thus learn why your hope can be limitless. God loved you with a personal love, before time began: "I have loved thee with an everlasting love" (Jer 31:3) was spoken of you as truly as it was of Israel. For, as you have seen, "before the foundation of the world He chose you out in Christ . . ." (Eph 1:4). Then, at the beginning of time He made the promise you have been studying, a promise that meant an everlasting life of love for you: "I will put enmities between thee and the woman . . ." (Gn 3:15). Then, in the fullness of time, He sent His only Son — who "loved you and gave himself up for you" (Gal 2:20).

What is presented here as personal between you and God is not a matter of clever reasoning; it is all revelation! Men may place a very low value on you as a person. You yourself may estimate your being as of little worth. But God's promise to Eve, and Gabriel's message to Mary, say that you are worth the very Blood of God — *"empti enim estis pretio magno"* (1 Cor 6:20). Most assuredly your purchase price was high! You cost God the pierced Heart of His only Son, and the broken heart of that Son's peerless Mother. But God the Father, who is infinitely wise, placed that price upon you.

To come to a clearer understanding of your ever contradictory self, look at Christ. He was perfectly human and perfectly divine. You are a Christian. You were born with a human nature. You were reborn and given a share in divine nature. That is revelation. "It is a fact," wrote St. Peter, "that his divine power has bestowed on us all needed aid for our spiritual life and piety, by imparting the deep knowledge of him who called us by his own glory and power. Through these manifestations he has bestowed on us precious and very great promises, to enable us to escape the corruption which lust causes in the world, and *become partakers of the divine nature"* (2 Pt 1:3, 4).

That we might know a share in this nature and thus be real Christians was one of the purposes of the Annunciation, because God is Love, and love craves union. Christ's high-priestly prayer at the Last Supper tells you how close a union Love desires with you, and me, and every other human being: "Holy Father, may they be one as we are one . . . just as you, Father, are in me and I am in you, so they, too, are to be one in us" (Jn 17:11–21).

There is our destiny. There, the goal of all our proper striving. There, too, is the source of the exultant joy in Christian life, and the unconquerable, irrepressible optimism in all true Christian living.

The Annunciation has lighted all the world's horizons with brightest hope. Men need to see that light; for without hope, men die. Life is a battle — for everyone; and in it, at one time or another, everyone is badly beaten. Hence, to go on with any enthusiasm, one must have faith and hope; one must believe that life has meaning, and he must hope that it really leads somewhere; that there is a goal to gain which will ultimately justify all the mysteriousness and incomprehensibility of life's often cruel and callous realities. Without such a hope the world is absurd, and human life folly.

We who have hope know the world is anything but absurd and human life far from folly. Where did we get our hope if not from the Annunciation? Let us study the anatomy of hope that we may love God the more. Hope, you know, is born of love. For, first, you see someone or something you in some way love; for that someone or something appeals to you as good. You desire to possess that good. It is between desire for and the possession of the object desired that your entire affective life lies. But between desire and possession there is often both distance and difficulty. If the distance seems too great, or the difficulties insurmountable, you despair of ever possessing the object. But, if on the contrary, you believe that you have, or can acquire, the means to surmount those difficulties and conquer the distance, hope comes into being. Not wishful thinking, understand, but well-grounded expectation of success, genuine hopefulness sets a person to work.

The hopeful man, then, is a man in love, who has not yet attained the object of his love. His whole being is oriented to the future; for his joy lies in the final acquisition of the good he desires. He is not smug, not complacent, not a satisfied man. For as yet he has not arrived. Rather, he is eager; for he is filled with certainty.

There is the paradox of hope. It lies in the fact that the hopeful man is certain even amid his uncertainties. His is not the calm confidence of one who simply has to bide his time, and the object of his desires will fall into his lap. He is one who has to fight his way to the possession of what he has set his heart upon. But he is sure that the means are at hand; sure that, even while facing the obstacles in his way, and realizing the uncertainties that surround his efforts, he can be confident of ultimate success — if he will but use the means. The heart of all true hope, then, lies in the nature of the means at hand to win one's way to the possession of his heart's desire.

With that before us, we can appreciate the mystery of the Annunciation the more; for we can see how Gabriel's message gives birth to what may be called the only genuine hope for man on earth. For, you see, the goal of life for every human is nothing less than the possession of God — and that for all eternity! The distance, between the desire in the heart of each of us and that possession of Him who is the Infinite Good, is itself quite definitely infinite. The obstacles, too, that lie between man and his attainment to God, are quite definitely insurmountable — without the means given through the Annunciation! For, ultimately speaking, this mystery gives us Christ — and "through Him, with Him, and in Him" man can attain the otherwise unattainable Good called God.

It is Christ who is announced in this mystery of the Annunciation, who is the real Foundation of all our genuine hope. That Christ became a Corpse. But that Corpse rose from the dead. That is why St. Peter could so triumphantly write: "Blessed be God the Father of our Lord Jesus Christ! Through his great mercy he has begotten us anew to a *living hope* through the resurrection of Jesus Christ from the dead. This hope is directed to the inheritance, imperishable, flawless, unfading, reserved for you in heaven. God's power guards you through your faith for the salvation that is held in readiness to be revealed at the end of time. Because of this you experience steadfast happiness, even though now for a little while you must be afflicted by various trials . . ." (1 Pt 1:3–6).

Hope, then, is a divine force. It comes from God. It is fire in your being. It is a flame no human misery can quench; for it is a heaven-born, living, irresistible reality. You need just such a fire, and it needs to flame; for you were born for glory — the glory of God. The means for attaining this seemingly unattainable Good is before your eyes — in the example of Mary.

Become what she became. Do what she did. Be a "humble servant of the Lord." Desire only that "all that has been said [of you] be fulfilled in you." Do you ask what it is that has been said of you? St. Paul tells you that you had been "chosen in Christ before the foundation of the world that you should be holy and without blemish in his sight. Out of love he has predestined you for himself to become through Jesus Christ his adopted child" (Eph 1:4, 5). He also drew for you the immediate consequences of this "annunciation" when he said you could "draw near with a sincere heart, in full assurance of faith, and cling without faltering to the hope you profess, for he who has given the promise is faithful" (Heb 10:22, 23). The Apostle tells you why your hope can be unfaltering: "when God gave his promise to Abraham, he swore by himself — there was none greater by whom to swear. In this way God wished to show more convincingly to the heirs of the promised blessing the irrevocable character of his plan. . . . Thus by two irrevocable assurances, where deceit on the part of God is impossible, we have great encouragement to take refuge in a firm grasp on the hope set before us. It is an anchor for the soul" (Heb 6:13–19).

God has done His part. He has not only promised, but, already, has kept part of that promise. For "God, who is rich in mercy, was moved by the intense love with which he loved us, and when we were dead by reason of our transgressions, he made us live with the life of Christ. By grace you have been saved. Together with Christ Jesus and in him, he has raised us up and enthroned us in the heavenly realm, that in Christ he might show throughout the ages to come the overflowing riches of his grace springing from his goodness to us. . . . We are his handiwork, created in Christ Jesus in view of the good deeds which God prepared beforehand for us to practice" (Eph 2:4–10).

We must do our part. It is outlined there by St. Paul — inspired by God Himself. We can hope as Abraham hoped. Indeed, we can outhope him. For we have almost infinitely more reasons for more hope than Abraham. We have two thousand years since Gabriel's Annunciation to Mary, and in each of them, in each day of them, we can find God being faithful to all His promises. We must do our part, I say; we must "practice the deeds God prepared beforehand for us to practice"; for "as yet your salvation is only a matter of hope" (Rom 8:24).

It is well to realize that hope is, so to speak, a link between faith and charity. Like faith, which is, in a way, naught but a waiting for the vision of God, hope is an awaiting for that full possession of the Object it loves and desires. Faith places us in the presence of God as it proposes Him to us as our supreme Good. It is thus that faith sets us loving God and desiring Him, not with an ineffectual wishing, but desiring with all the fire of our being to possess Him. This is no groundless aspiration on our part; for God has promised us eternal possession of Himself. But He asks of us what He asked of Mary — complete trust, wholehearted abandonment to His Will. Once we really make our wills one with His, life holds no difficulty that cannot be overcome.

What could fire our hope more intensely than these words of St. Paul: "Those whom he has predestined, he has called; and those whom he has called, he has sanctified; and those whom he has sanctified, he has glorified" (Rom 8:30). If we but yield ourselves to God "in Christ Jesus" we will walk, step by step, as Paul has outlined here, and walk on to Glory.

Christ, obviously, is the key to all the mysteries in your life. Live your life "in Christ Jesus" and, unquestionably, you will pass through all the mysteries in the life of Christ. The "annunciation" Gabriel never made, as well as the one he actually made, was a call to you — and your call to the Faith can justly be named your own personal "annunciation."

In looking at the two corpses found at the opening of your story, you are, in a very certain way, looking at yourself. Abel tells of sin. Christ tells of salvation. You, a sinner, have been redeemed. Redemption should lead on to salvation! It will if you live "in Christ Jesus." Abel tells you of one nature that you possess. You are quite conscious of it. It has a darkened intellect, a weakened will, three concupiscences, and seven capital sins. In one sense, it is a nature that could nauseate. But see how God has offset all imbalance with grace, which is the very life of God — a share in His nature — within you, light for that darkened intellect, strength for that weakened will. With it came three theological virtues that outbalance the three concupiscences. And the seven Gifts of the Holy Spirit, which you also received, impel you toward God with greater force than the seven capital sins incline you to evil. So, hope! Rejoice and be glad! God is within you. You aready possess Him by faith and love. Let your hope that you will possess Him forever soar. Let it grow stronger with each ringing of the *Angelus* bell.

The sound of that bell can free you from every fear; for it reminds you of that annunciation which Gabriel did make, and can now stir you to remembrance of the one he did not make. Both of those annunciations had to do with Christ — and He has overcome the world! "In Him, through Him, and with Him," you are to do the same. He who is the Lord of life is not only the beginning and center of history, but also its final end. Day by day, hour by hour, His Kingdom comes, not only despite the madness of your world and the persecution by the wicked, but even because of that madness and through that persecution. You are helping that Kingdom to come. That makes life worth living — and death worth dying.

Let the *Angelus* bell tell you that it is not "the divinity of the bomb" that broods over our world, but the love of God. In the words of Gerard Manley Hopkins: ". . . the Holy Ghost over the bent world broods with warm breast and with, Ah! bright wings."

For that bell tells you that "God so loved the world that he gave his only Son for it." It tells you that God became Man; that God is the Lord of the Universe — which will become "a new heaven and a new earth" when, and in the way He has predetermined — not as man devises!

That *Angelus* bell will help solve the mysteries in your life as it fills you with hope and with that love which "casts out fear." It will also sound a challenge for you *to become what you are!*

*CHAPTER FOUR*

# This Mystery Tells You Your Mission in Life

~~~~~~~~~~~~~~~~~~~~~~~~~~~~~~~~~~~~~~~~~~~~~~~~~~~~~~~~~~

*Become What You Are*

MOST of our life is lived on the surface. We allow ourselves simply to drift along from day to day, played upon by countless external forces: political, social, economic, physical; pulled this way and that, also, by numerous internal forces: thought, imagination, emotion, passion, hunger, thirst, desire. Seldom do we stop and look down into the deep, and ever deepening abyss whence all these interior forces arise and whence come our reactions to them. That is why so few of us know just what our "selfhood" is; who we really are; what this thing we call "life" actually is; or what "living" requires.

No physical science will reveal to you the origin, the nature, the character of that force which enables you to think, love, and be. You can search back through all your ancestors, but you will never discover among any of them, not even in the original sire of your particular "clan," the source of your being. For that, you will have to go back beyond the corpse found in the beginning of this book, that of the first man who ever died. You will have to go back and back until you come face to face with the One who created Adam and Eve. That is the One who looks up at you as you look down into the depths to your "selfhood" — God.

When you look back to the surface of life again, you will only open your eyes to even greater mystery: How is it that among the myriad enemies to life and living, you have managed to survive? Death is all around you — has always been; yet you continue to be; you have not died. Why? — There is only one satisfying answer. It is the same that you found concerning the question

33

of your source of life: God. He made you a participant in being. He continues to sustain you in being. He molded you to His own image and likeness just as surely as He molded the first man. He breathed life into you just as surely as He breathed life into Adam. There is no other source of life. In all truth, you are in the hands of God. Were not those two hands sustaining you this very moment, you would cease both to live and to be. You are not only one whom God produced; you are one He is still producing. That is your "selfhood": *a continuing work of God.* He commanded you to be; He is still commanding you to go on becoming — becoming what you are; becoming yourself. Your response to those commands is both your life and your living. Therein you see life's most real duty. You must become what you are — or fail to have lived!

*Become what you are* is a command that gives everyone and anyone pause. We ask: What does it actually mean? The answer to that question means life.

*Become what you are* is not a contradiction. Rather, the admonition holds the one real challenge of life and to living. More, it holds the fundamental command of nature — or better, of nature's God.

*Become what you are.* You are human. You were born such. But have you become fully human as yet? You are a man or a woman. You came into life such. But have you become the man you are capable of becoming? Have you lived life manfully all your years? Or if you are a woman, have you lived in the manner ever becoming to your sex or the woman who is your ideal?

*Become what you are.* We *are.* But we are not yet what we shall be. We are still *becoming.* To be means always to be becoming, and to live means to go on becoming different. So long as we exist there is, there can be, nothing static about us. We are always becoming — better or worse. Life is active; and that activity always shows us becoming — better or worse. There is no imperious necessity for all of us to become mental prodigies; no urgent necessity for each of us to attain the highest rank in social or political life; no pressing need for all of us to become financial wizards, economic tycoons. But there is inescapable need for each one of us to become what we are by Baptism. We must become what we are — we are *Christ,* made so by that Sacrament.

So now the command "Become what you are!" takes on eternal import, as it is seen to be an imperative that connotes life's only success, and life's only absolute failure. It tells us that we are, and intimates that as yet we are not all that we can be. We have being — the very being of God within us. For we were incorporated into Christ at Baptism as St. Paul so vigorously insists: "We were buried in death with him [Christ] by means of Baptism, *in order that* just as Christ was raised from the dead by the glorious power of the Father, so we may also conduct ourselves by *a new principle of life*" (Rom 6:3–5). That new principle of life is the Christ-principle; that new life is the Christ-life. Since action takes on the nature of the being, you see how inescapable is the conclusion that to become what we are we must become Christ.

In the Prologue to his Gospel, St. John sets it down as incontestable that "to as many as welcomed him [Christ] he gave the power to become the children of God — those who believe in his name; who were born not of blood or of carnal desire, or of man's will; no, they were *born of God*" (1:12, 13). Since those who are born of men are human, it follows that those who are "born of God" must be divine. That theological truth you have already been presented with by the first Vicar of Christ, and the very "rock" of His Church. St. Peter told you that God has made us "partakers of the divine nature." *Become what you are,* can mean only one thing: you must become divine!

It was Socrates who said: "An unexamined life is not worth living." The fact that he made that remark just before he was condemned to death adds force to his observation. When you recall that he was asking for an examination into *virtuous* living and into the *virtuous* life, you will see how Christian is this remark of a non-Christian. The life of a Christian, which is "unexamined," is most assuredly not worth living; for it in no sense is a real life.

Look into yourself. Realize that you are one who has been set by God into two distinct solidarities: one with Adam, the other with Christ. By your human birth you were set in the solidarity of sin. By your divine birth, through Baptism, you were set in the solidarity of sanctity. Your name is Christ. You are holy with the holiness of God. But your name is also Cain. . . .

We are back to the two corpses again. But we are in a new mystery in your life: *The Visitation.*

Undoubtedly it will strike you as strange that this mystery, which St. Luke so vividly describes in his Gospel, and which seems a mystery involving two pregnant women and their unborn sons, should now be presented to you as a mystery in *your* life. But that striking strangeness is only proof that you, like too many others, have taken *being* a Christian as something finished once and for all, and not as it is in all reality: a continuing process, a steady *becoming what you are.* To be a Catholic is to be personally involved in the unfinished Drama of Salvation; to be a participant in that Christ-centered reality begun in Eden when God told Satan He would place "enmity between him and the woman, between his seed and hers, and that she should crush his head." That drama still goes on. It will end only when "the sun will darken, the moon cease to shed her light." For it is only then that "the sign of the Son of Man will appear in the sky" — and you will win divine applause — or divine condemnation — for the way you have played your role as a member of Christ in this drama which fills all time, and whose cast is made up of God and all mankind. When that "sign of the Son of Man" does appear, you will be rewarded or condemned for the way you have lived the mysteries in your life, and most particularly this mystery of the Visitation.

The facts of the mystery as lived by Mary and Jesus in their lifetime are well known. After Gabriel had made that annunciation to Mary at Nazareth, he told her that her relative, Elizabeth, had conceived a son in her old age, and was then "in her sixth month." Then St. Luke goes on to narrate how "Mary set out in haste to go into the mountains to visit a town of Juda." Think of all that is contained in this simply stated fact! Mary, the Maid of Nazareth, is aglow with God. She had just been overshadowed by the Power of the Most High. She had just conceived God by God. She is filled to overflowing with Love. But love, when it is true love, must act. Joy must communicate itself. Goodness must always go out of itself and give to others. That is why Mary hurried off into the hills. She would literally carry God into the house of her cousin, Elizabeth.

But what have you been made by Baptism? Once those transforming waters touched your head, you, too, had God within you. You, too, had become a Christ-bearer. You, too, were set aglow with God. From that moment on, your life should have been naught but a "visitation"; for you should have gone forth carrying Christ within you, and affecting those whom you greeted as Elizabeth was affected by Mary's salutation that happy day in Ain Karin.

Too often we look upon the Incarnation merely as the coming of God into flesh. It was that. It still is that; for Jesus Christ still lives in the same flesh He took from the flesh of Mary, His Mother. It is in a glorified state now, yet it is the selfsame flesh. But the Incarnation was not only the coming of God into flesh; it was — and still is — the going out of God to men of flesh and blood. That is why there was a Visitation immediately after the Annunciation. God was spurring Mary on to *carry Him to others.*

God always takes the initiative. Every supernatural act — the only kind of act that befits men and women who have been redeemed — has God as its Author; for it is always divine in origin. The response of the human, and the total effect of the corporate act, follows on God's lead. He is "The Hound of Heaven" who follows us "down the nights and down the days." He is the Good Shepherd who is ever seeking out His strays. He is the Good Samaritan ever binding up someone's wounds. He is the loving Father of the Prodigal, ever awaiting His son's return. He is the Criminal on the central Cross ever speaking pardon and promising Paradise to the thief on His right — and longing, with all the love of His infinitely loving Heart, for the thief on His left to recognize Him for who He is — Love.

The Visitation of Mary to Elizabeth was the first going out of God to sanctify men. God was then but a tiny creature in the virginal womb of a very young girl; yet He was Love. And Love

must act. He spurs Mary on to Ain Karin that He might sanctify
the child stirring with six months' life beneath the aged heart of
Zachary's wife, Elizabeth.

See how dependent the eternally independent and omnipotent
God is on His weak creatures of time. He needed that little
Jewish girl, Mary, to carry Him to the home of Zachary that He
might there sanctify John the Baptist and set him leaping with
glad holiness in the womb of his mother. Now "Jesus Christ is
the same yesterday, today, and forever" (Heb 13:8). Therefore,
He is as dependent on you today as He was on Mary in that
yesterday of long ago. You can carry Him to those He would
sanctify. Your life can be one long, uninterrupted "visitation" if
you will *become what you are.*

Many a man, and many a woman, has lamented the seeming
emptiness and all-too-obvious meaninglessness of their lives. Who
can blame them so long as it is the surface of reality that is seen,
and the mysteries that lie below that surface never glimpsed? Just
look at the ordinary man or woman of today. Does not life seem
to be made up of a multitude of trifles for them? Does not their
life look meaningless and empty?

As with the ordinary man and woman so with the so-called
extraordinary. Life and living, when viewed on the surface, are
much the same for all — and equally meaningless. To silence any
challenge to that statement, let it be known that of the billions
on billions of humans who have lived, loved, suffered, and died
on this earth of ours, a scant five thousand names are found on
the rolls of the professional historians as humans who have
achieved "immortality." And who knows even the names of most
of these so-called immortals save the professional historians?

Yet, all of us have "intimations of immortality." There is in all
of us a need for work, for creative work, for work that is meaningful. In each of us is an ineradicable craving to accomplish; not
only to accomplish, but to accomplish something lasting; to contribute something to the well-being of our fellowmen, to make
some kind of a contribution to society. But in a world ruled largely
by materialistic philosophy, and in a society that is, for the most
part, "acquisitive," what contribution can Christian man make?

Novelist J. D. Salinger has one of his characters sum up life in this mid-twentieth century by saying: "Everything everyone does is so tiny, and meaningless, and sad-making." Too sweeping a statement, of course. Too easy a generalization. Yet, when we look back from our century of great achievements, and scrutinize the past for mortal man's immortal accomplishments, we usually find ourselves ending up in El Gizeh, in Upper Egypt, looking upon the everlasting pyramids, and gazing up into the ever quizzical smile of the sphinx. These are mortal man's immortal achievements. Noisy centuries upon noisy centuries have passed into the silence of history since these magnificent structures were first set above Egypt's soil. Yet, with all their seeming timelessness, what do they really signify? Do they actually mean any more than the "tiny, meaningless, sad-making" things of our twentieth century that so distressed Franny in Salinger's *Franny and Zooey?*

Life does give the thinking man and woman reason to pause and ask: "What is the meaning of it all?" Especially is this true when we look at youth. Here are the ones who will fall heirs to what we older people accomplish or acquire. Here are the ones who will take our present and our past, and make the future. But acute observers tell us that youth is weary. Contradiction though it seems, youth is weary: weary of life, of society, of education, of civilization; weary of politics, both national and international; weary of everything and everyone, even — and often especially — of themselves. And it is inevitable that they will grow more weary as long as they look only at the surface, and never beneath and discover the mysteries that make up their life — most especially this mystery of the Visitation.

Consider the actors in this mystery as it was lived in the long ago: a young maiden hurries into the hill country to visit an aged cousin who is expecting a child after many sad years of sterility. On the surface, two more ordinary people could hardly be found. Mary's youth and beauty might draw a second glance. But not Elizabeth's, Zachary's aged wife. Yet, when the pyramids have crumbled to dust and the smile of the sphinx is but a legend, generations will go on hailing Mary, echoing Elizabeth's words: "Blessed are you beyond all women! And blessed is the fruit of your womb!" Until the end of time men, women, and little children will be repeating in their hearts the words Zachary's wife spoke that memorable day: "How privileged I am to have the mother of my Lord come to visit me!" For that young Maiden-Mother will go on visiting souls spiritually just as she visited Ain Karin physically, so long as there will be souls in need of sanctification, as was the soul of the unborn Baptist. Mary, carrying Christ beneath her heart, did one of the truly immortal works of mankind that day — and you have been blessed by God with the identical mission. You have been predestined by God to carry Christ within you — and to bring Him into the presence of the born and the as yet unborn. Your life is meant to be one long "visitation"; for you have been made a Christ-bearer by Baptism just as really — although mystically — as Mary was made the day she was over-shadowed by the Holy Spirit after the Annunciation.

You want to contribute something genuinely beneficial to your fellowman. You want to achieve a work that will last, accomplish something that will live on after you have left this earth. You will — if you will *become what you are*. You will — if you awake to the mystery that is the Visitation. Be the Christ-bearer you were made to be, and you will give the deepest possible meaning to your days on earth, even as you make your living effective for eternity, not only for yourself, but for others.

Few of us totally dependent mortals ever realize how truly dependent upon us is the only immortal and independent God. Jesus Christ, Son of God, true God of true God, came to earth and revealed Himself to mankind as the Way, the Truth, and the Life. But that was long, long ago. He left this earth physically in the earliest part of the first century. How, then, are the men and women of this twentieth century ever to find the Way, learn the Truth, live the Life? — *You* are the answer!

What makes Jesus Christ attractive — or repulsive — to the men and women of our century? Not the preaching done by the ministers of God — nor the castigations of Him by His enemies. Not the writings of gifted authors for or against the Christ. Not the splendor of ecclesiastical art and architecture, nor the modern iconoclastic attacks upon them. What makes Jesus Christ attractive — or repulsive — is *the life led by His members*.

The non-Christian Mahatma Gandhi, once said that he liked our Christ, but that he disliked our Christians because they were so unlike our Christ. A similar condemnation came from the pen of a Christian. As he sat in the cell of a Nazi prison awaiting the sentence of death, Father Delp wrote: "We [Christians] have destroyed man's confidence in us by the way we live."

We are Christ's members. To have destroyed man's confidence in us, is to have destroyed man's confidence in Christ. That is the crime of all crimes. For it means that we have blocked the Way, distorted the Truth, perverted, if we have not prevented, the Life from reaching other men.

Of course we can hope that Father Delp's conclusion is not universally true; that it is not applicable in full force to all Catholics and all Christians. And we have substantial reasons for believing it is not. Nevertheless, his line does give us all reason to examine our lives and look sharply into our living.

That searing line could never have been written if all baptized persons realized that, by their very Baptism, they were given a mission which is recognized for what it is in this mystery of the Visitation. We have been made Christ-bearers. When we are in what is called "the state of grace," we carry Christ with us no matter where we go. Hence, all our goings in and all our goings out take on the splendor of the Visitation; for God is as near to us when we are in the state of grace as ever He was to Mary when she set out to visit Elizabeth. He is one with us.

That must be accepted on the word of The Word. At the Last Supper Christ promised the unbelievable: "Anyone who loves me," said this Son of God become the Son of Man, "will treasure my message, and my Father will love him, and we shall visit him and make our home with him." God, Father, Son, and Holy Spirit, come and make their home in him who loves God. That is the explicit reality promised by Christ Jesus. So it is not with probabilities we are dealing, not with daring dreams, but with fact. The Indwelling of the Trinity is as actual and factual as is the presence of Christ in the transubstantiated Host. Our belief in this reality is based on the word of The Word. Christ said so. That suffices.

Paul taught this doctrine to his Corinthians — and it is well to recall the milieu from which the Corinthian Christians came, and in which they lived. Corinth of old, like Paris, London, Chicago, or New York today, was materially prosperous, and morally corrupt. "To live like a Corinthian" was the way the people of those days described a profligate. What was the safeguard Paul offered Christians in such a milieu? — The realization of what God had done to them: "he who unites himself to the Lord, forms one spirit with him," wrote the Apostle. Then added: "Are you not aware that your body is the temple of the Holy Spirit? Him you have received from God! . . . So then, glorify the God in your body" (1 Cor 6:17–20).

*Glorify God* . . . that is the one ultimate work everyone has in life. Do that one work and life has been a success. Do that one work and you *become what you are;* for you have been "predestined to be devoted to the praise of his glory" (Eph 1:12). Further, "the final purpose of being sealed (with the promised Spirit) is our redemption as God's possession to the praise of his glory" (Eph 1:14).

To become what we are, we must steadily become an ever greater "praise of God's glory." That is precisely what Paul meant when he told his Corinthians to "glorify God in your body." It was not only for themselves the Apostle would quicken this God-consciousness, but for those among whom they lived. In this he was but echoing the earliest teaching of Christ. In His Sermon on the Mount, Christ had said: "So let your light shine before your fellow men, that they may see your good example and praise your Father who is in heaven" (Mt 5:16). Peter urged the same: "See that your conduct among pagans is praiseworthy . . . so that they may come to a better appreciation of your praiseworthy deeds and glorify God when he grants them conversion" (1 Pt 2:12).

Ever and always it is: *to glorify God.* No matter where you look in the New Testament, whether in the Gospels, Epistles, Acts, or the Apocalypse, the mission of man is always stated the same way: *to glorify God*. For that was the first and the final purpose of creation. In the Old Testament the Psalmist tells you that "the very heaven tells the glory of God" (Ps 18:1). The sun, moon, stars, earth, and sea do the same. But it is only man who can give God formal glory — from earth and time — and you are a man living on earth in time. *Become what you are* — you were made to be a living praise of God's glory; not by words and deeds only, but by your very being. That is your deepest "selfhood." You have been created to be a pulsing "Glory be to the Father — and to the Son — and to the Holy Spirit." Yours is the call to become an animated Doxology. Do that and your life and living will be the mystery of the Visitation lived over again; and you will be employed in the greatest work possible to man: you will be doing what the angels do in Heaven, and more; for you will not only be glorifying God, you will be sanctifying your fellowman as you go about carrying God to others.

That is what Mary did at Ain Karin. Commentators on this mystery point out that it was God who moved Mary to this work of love. Who will question the comment after what we have seen about God always taking the initiative in such works, and what we have learned about love being born of God and God being Love?

The commentators point out also that this was, perhaps, the happiest time of Mary's life. Joseph had noticed nothing physically different about his spouse, so there was no worry in his mind or questioning light in his eyes. Bethlehem had closed no doors as yet. The manger was ready. God saw to that. But Mary had no idea that she would bring forth her Child in a cattle cave. Herod's sword slept in its scabbard. Simeon had not yet uttered his prophecy about the "sign of contradiction" or about the piercing of the Immaculate Heart. Hence there was nothing but sunshine and song about this mystery.

So should it be for all who live it out in our day. Just as Mary was aglow with God as she saluted Elizabeth, so are all we who are in "the state of grace." That one fact is enough to flood anyone's world with sunshine and quicken it to life with song:

God — the Three-Personed Infinite God — dwells in us! No Wonder Chesterton said: "Joy is the secret of Christianity." Not only joy about the past — joy in the fact that we have been redeemed. Not only joy about the future — joy in the fact that it is God's Will that we all be saved. But very especially joy in the present — joy in the fact that Christ's high-priestly prayer is answered: We are one with God as Father and Son are One! Alive with God! Who would not jump for joy — leap as did the Baptist? And that is our role in life.

Clare Boothe Luce once described a Catholic as "a person who, when accosted by anyone and asked so little a question as the correct time, would make the questioner conscious that he or she had come in contact with a person who was alive with God, aglow with His glory, radiant of Jesus Christ."

Let me cite from a letter I received just a few days ago from a young convert of mine who went on safari to East Africa. She had been in Kenya, Tanganyika, and Uganda and had seen many of God's wonderful animals. After that she went to the Congo looking for gorillas. Came Sunday, and she wanted to assist at Mass. She learned of a mission some three miles from where she had struck camp and persuaded her white hunter to drive her there. After Mass she came out of the chapel and met what she described as "some fantastic White Sisters who run a leper colony here. Even my great White Hunter, who sulked all the way over to the Mission, was struck by the dedication that adorns their every word and gesture. The one who stole my heart — and even his! — is French. She stands about four feet, eight; is sixty-five years old — looks thirty — and has been out here for seventeen years. She is more vibrantly alive with God than any person I have ever met. Two years ago, when the uprising was at its fiercest, she *alone* saved the lives of four priests, eight nuns, and all the black workers in the Mission. Just twelve miles away six nuns and all the priests in the parish were killed. She has that intangible 'something,' which can only be defined as 'humanized divinity.' How I wish you could meet her. She alone is in charge of three hundred lepers. When she smiles her whole being lights up with what I know is God."

Perhaps you have been in the presence of some aged nun who had given her entire life to God, or some old, serenely kind pastor who is but waiting God's final summons Home, and wondered what it was that made the atmosphere different. It was God — God within them. They were living the Visitation! After you left them you could have said what the French peasant said after his return from Ars where he had visited the village Curé — John Baptist Vianney: "Today, I saw God in a man." That is what people ought to be able to say after meeting you; and they will be enabled to do so if you live conscious of your mission in life — the same mission that sent Mary into the hill country.

We are not too alert to the supernatural in our present day; but that is no proof that God is not near, is not operative in our culture and civilization, is not dwelling in and being dynamic in us. Whence the love that suffuses the face of any modern madonna? Whence the love light in the eyes of her child? "Love is born of God." Not only the love that radiates from them, but the very life that is manifest in them, shows you God present in our world. For God, the Author of life, not only gives life, He sustains it. Creation demands continual creation. God is breathing in that mother and in that child — else they could not breathe. Like organ notes — they will have life in them only so long as God, who is at the console, holds His fingers on the keys.

You can see God in action as you look on the wise ways of uneducated parents. How can you account for the wisdom they show? It is not difficult if you have pondered the marvel of Baptism. It is not only the Gift of the Holy Spirit operative in such parents, it is the Holy Spirit Himself who was their Gift. What we so often call sagacity is actually very often actual sanctity. Recalling that line of the *Gloria* which says of Christ: "Thou only art holy," we can conclude that sanctity is God present and operative in a soul. Then what we have so often called goodness we will now call God.

Analyze the happening at Ain Karin — John's leaping within his mother's womb — and you will see the greatness of the work that is yours as you go about radiating Christ. The unborn Baptist leaped with joy because he had been baptized, as it were, by Mary's breath. At her salutation the shackles of original sin fell from his soul, and he was lifted, while still in his mother's womb, to the heights of supernatural vitality. Christ Himself would say later that He had come to earth that men "might have life, and have it more abundantly" (Jn 10:10). Not ordinary human life; for men already had that. But a share in His own divine vitality. Live your mystery of your "visitation" and you will be a carrier of divine vitality to others, set them leaping with joy, and the air about you ringing with song.

"Song," said St. Augustine, "belongs to the lover." Just think of all the song there was at Ain Karin that day of Mary's Visitation — and of all the prayer. Elizabeth gave us the continuation of the Angelical Salutation: "Blessed art thou among women, and blessed is the fruit of thy womb . . ." Mary gave us the song of her soul, which should be the love song, and joy song of our lives: *Magnificat* — "My soul extols the Lord; and my spirit leaps for joy in God, my Saviour. . . . How sublime is what He has done for me — the Mighty One, whose name is 'Holy.' " Zachary, the father of John the Baptist, broke his heaven-sent silence with that reverence-filled *Benedictus* — another song to lighten all life's burdens: "Blessed be the Lord, the God of Israel! He has visited his people and brought about its redemption."

*Prayer* — is there enough of it in our lives? Our Lord tells us that we "ought always to pray" (Lk 18:1). Could it be that we are not becoming what we are simply because we have neglected that directive? Have we failed to realize that prayer is a necessity for all our living? What are we but mendicants with arms outstretched begging God for the next breath and heartbeat? We have no title to them. Each comes as a gift from the Giver of all gifts, who told us that we are to ask, and we shall receive. Why is it that we do not ask sufficiently?

We learn from this mystery of the Visitation just what should be the burden of our prayer. It should be praise of God first. Magnify Him as Mary did. Bless Him as Zachary did. Exclaim in grateful wonder about His goodness as Elizabeth did. Then we can go on and ask for ourselves. The Christ, as He did to the Baptist, will set us "jumping with joy." It was He who taught us how to pray by telling us that when we pray we should say: "Our Father . . ." Yes, God *is* our Father. We should show ourselves His trusting children and ask that His name be hallowed, that His Kingdom come, that His Will be done. Then we can ask for our daily bread, for forgiveness, for protection against those temptations that may be real obstacles to our becoming what we are: Christophers who carry Christ to others, thus making our lives what they are supposed to be: veritable "visitations."

The late Father Vincent McNabb, O.P., was fond of telling young priests how he had been advised by an expert spiritual guide not to be too severe with those who accused themselves of grave sins of the flesh, but to "raise a row," as he phrased it, with those who neglected their prayers. Neglect of prayer tells of a faith that is worse than weak; an idea of God that is entirely faulty; and a concept of self that is completely wrong. For we are creatures who need God every split second of our existence.

Do not say that it is difficult to pray; for the truth is that it is difficult *not* to pray. There are countless ways to pray. The fact is that there is nothing in your life that cannot be turned into prayer — save sin. Sin cannot be offered to God. But everything else in your life can be — and this offering, which can be continuous, constitutes prayer. The unlearned and unwise may say that the duties of your state in life keep you from prayer. What a fallacy! The duties of your state in life are manifestly the Will of God for you, and one of the fundamental petitions taught us by God Himself is: "Thy will be done." Therefore, when the duties of one's state in life are carried out because they are the Will of God and offered to Him as such, they constitute one of the most fundamental forms of prayer, a form which can enable us to follow that directive of Christ: "Pray always" (Lk 18:1).

Distinguish clearly between *saying* prayers and *praying,* and you have solved the whole fallacious difficulty. A mother cleaning her home is praying if she has offered her day to God, and is cleaning the home because she knows that is the Will of God for her at the moment. The father out working is praying all the time he labors so long as he has offered it all to God, and recognizes work as the Will of God for him. Of course this is not the only form of prayer, but it is one of the essential forms for those who would become what they are; for, ultimately, we, in our very being, are to become a prayer, since prayer is "union with God." That union is had in mind and will; for it is the mind and will that really make us human.

All of us know how difficult it is to keep from thinking of one we love. "Out of sight, out of mind" is not true about parted lovers. Well, if prayer can be somewhat loosely, but in no way inaccurately, defined as "thinking of God," you can see why I say it is difficult *not* to pray. You can also see why I say that if we pray little, we have very good reason to look into the quality of our love for God. If we are alive with love for God we cannot keep from praying; and since we cannot keep from praying we are always united with Him, and thus are always living our "visitation."

But we must ever be mindful of the fact that we carry Christ about in us not only for the purpose exhibited at Ain Karin, but even more especially for the purpose Mary carried Him within her when she headed for Bethlehem: we want Christ to know birth — *in others!* Hence, the mystery of the "visitation" in your life leads you on to another, deeper mystery — one that is the center of all the other mysteries in your life, and, in its own way, their solution: the mystery of the *Incarnation*.

# CHAPTER FIVE

# This Mystery Solves All Other Mysteries

*"Listen: I Am Bringing You Good News . . ."*

THE problem creature of earth is, and always has been, *man*. He is not only a problem; he is, as we have already seen, a mystery. But he is one mystery best solved by keeping him face to face with the unfathomable Mystery we call God.

We of the twentieth century are fortunate in that we live at a time when God shines before us with exceptional clarity. That is true despite militant atheism, widespread neopaganism, and the blindness of many of our all-seeing scientists and would-be educators. Today there is no possibility of confusing God, as so many of our forefathers did, with the "gods of nature"; no possibility of associating Him with what the ancients called demiurges or "lesser gods"; no probability of our going up to "the groves" or the "high hills" for worship, or of our sacrificing to the rivers, the skies, or the forests. We know that "Nature" is not God; that images are images and nothing more; that God is the Great Alone, the utterly Other. Today we know that to this lone Transcendant all men are responsible; that to Him we must give a definite "yes" or a definite "no"; that with Him there is no possibility of straddling or of compromise. We have clarity about being with Him or against Him.

Two thousand years ago, in one of the caves that stand in the chalk hills outside Bethlehem, a Boy was born. The birth of a boy on this earth of ours was nothing new. Many other boys had no doubt been born in caves. But the birth of this Boy in that cave outside Bethlehem not only changed all human births from then on until the last human will be born, but had retroactive effect on every human birth back to that of Cain from Eve and Adam. For with Him a new race of men was born. Through Him, and in Him, and because of Him man could be man only by being more than man. The mystery of this Boy's birth is called the Incarnation. The name is descriptive; for it tells that God "became flesh"; that God became man; that Divinity became human, and the Alone "dwelt among us."

This mystery sheds such bright light on man that we can now say that the indefinable can be defined, the unintelligible readily understood, and the indescribable described. Man, as a mystery, is far less mysterious, thanks to the unfathomable mystery of God becoming Man.

In this study of the mysteries in your life you have looked upon Eve holding the body of the first man ever to die and Mary with the Corpse of God's only Son in her lap. You are now at the point where you can fashion a key that will unlock the mystery of your life and all the mysteries in your living of it. You will do that fashioning if you will now look again upon these two women with their sons in their arms, this time, however, as *Madonnas:* young mothers with their very young children at their breasts. See Eve as she hugs the firstborn of the human race to her heart in the wonder and thrill of the first human birth. Look at Mary as she holds the "firstborn of many brethren" to her Immaculate Heart, and adores her God in the Child of her womb. These two women are your mothers. From one you knew physical birth; from the other, spiritual generation. Since heredity is a fact, you can learn much about yourself as you look carefully not only at your mothers, but also at your brothers — the first in each strain: Cain and Christ.

Imagine what Eve must have thought as she held Cain in her arms. She had lived in "the Garden." She had "walked with God" as we may legitimately suppose, just as Adam had, "in the evening air." She had known domination over all animals. She had been truly "Queen of the Universe"; for, with Adam, she had been set as the "visible crown of God's visible creation." But then . . .

To look down on the child she had just brought forth "in sorrow," as God had foretold, and realize that she had been God's helpmate in producing human life, must have filled Eve with awe and adoration of God and His plans for humans. It must also have filled her with ecstatic wonder at the human who had issued from her womb according to God's plan. But, then, as she thought on about the life she could have given this child had she not listened to Satan, she had to look on her firstborn and know that, marvellous as he actually was, how much more marvellous he would have been had she held fast to God's original plan and been humbly obedient. She must have known that in the being of the child she held to her heart there was something very wrong; and that it was all her fault.

She knew he would not live in "the Garden" where first she had lived. For before it stood an angel with a flaming sword preventing reentrance.

She knew her son would never "walk with God in the afternoon air."

She must have realized that her son's mind would not be as bright as her own had been when she first looked at God, knew her own husband, and looked out with clear-seeing eyes on all God's wondrous creation. Nor would his will be as strong as hers had been when first the Serpent had asked her: "Why hath God commanded you, that you should not eat of every tree in paradise?" (Gn 3:1.) Darkened intellect and weakened will would be his. This last frightened her more than the first; for she well knew where freedom of will could lead one when wrongly used. She must have worried about the will her son would have with which to hold in check the fires of concupiscence which had flamed within her since that day of disobedience, with which to establish some order in the microcosm that was her son.

Eve must have known that the child to whom she had just given birth would know battle within himself and battle outside himself so long as he lived on earth — and all this warring would be his because she, his mother, had violated the order that had reigned within that "Garden"; had used her freedom in such a way that it would take the omnipotence of God to enable man once again to gain mastery so that body would be subject to soul, and soul would be obedient to God. Perhaps Eve did not know that God would have to become man before man could ever again become himself, but she had heard a clear promise, which was, in its way, an unconditioned promulgation of the decree of the Incarnation.

Try to enter Eve's thoughts as she sits holding her child — especially those about the heritage she had deprived that child of, and the lifelong struggle to which she had committed him, because of her dallying with the Tempter, and finally yielding to his suggestion. She ate the fruit that she might "be as God." That was the original temptation; that is the basis of practically every temptation; and it may well be man's final temptation as time ends. But you will learn even more about yourself if you will turn from the first Eve to the "second," and think theologically about her and her Child as she adores Him and loves Him at Bethlehem. Just as Eve knew there was something "wrong" with the child to whom she had given birth, so Mary was even more clearly conscious that there was something "new" about the Child she had just brought forth. With Him there was born a new race of men — or, rather, in Him the race of man was reborn.

As was said above that, thanks to the birth of Christ, the indefinable could be defined, the unintelligible understood, and the indescribable clearly described. We meant you and every man. When we glibly define man as "a composite of body and soul," we do man an injustice. Man, every man, any man, is ever so much more than body and soul; each is, and each will ever be, so long as he breathes on earth, body, soul, *and God*. To be, to have existence, establishes a necessary relation to Him who is — to God — to the Divine. That is true of a stone, a shrub, a song sparrow. It is preeminently truer of man. That is why man is undefinable. He is ever so much more than body and soul, or even a "rational animal." Man, *as a whole*, has a metaphysical nature. Too often we think it is only his soul that has such a nature. But man is not his soul, any more than he is his body. Recently it has been stated that man is a "personal possibility of a metaphysical realization."

That sounds profound, but all it means is that, by his very nature, man points beyond himself. We all know this from personal experience. We are never fully satisfied. Nor will we be, so long as we are on earth. There is no "natural fulfillment" for man —

which is very close to saying that man, by nature, is not natural. And that is precisely what Mary and her Son can tell you.

Perhaps it will clarify the point if we say that man's true destiny is *not* to become a man. The human was never meant to be *merely* human. In the beginning God decided to create man "in his own image." And He would place man "in a garden" where He might commune with him. God did just that. In other words, from what we know of creation, it is evident that God made man that the *two might be together*. Besides giving man being, God gave him the power to love and understand Him, the Divine Being. That can mean but one thing: God made man to participate personally in the intimate life of God, which means that man was made originally to live a supernatural life. That was his very "nature." That is what the ontological reality of man is: he needs God to fulfill himself; before he can be the man God made him to be, he must be more than man.

We see man as he should be when we look at Adam walking with God in the evening air. The child we see on Eve's breast — the firstborn of all men — has much of God in him; for he has a body and soul which came from God, and he lives only because the living God gave him life and continues to sustain him in living. Yet this child will never know the life his parents knew before they committed the original sin, which lost original justice for every man, and wounded human nature.

We often catch ourselves asking: "Why in the world did I do such a thing?" or "What is wrong with me, anyhow?" You have the answers to those questions as you look at Eve as the world's first *Madonna,* and think theologically about her firstborn. Cain can tell you what is wrong with you. He can tell you why you do those puzzling things, too. For in you is the same "wrongness" we found Eve conscious of as she thought of the legacy she could have handed on to her children — but lost in what we have come to call "the Fall." That Fall bruised every child of woman save that other Madonna and that other Firstborn Child. Now look at Mary and her Child and learn more about who you are!

St. Paul never tired of telling his Corinthians, Colossians, Galatians, Ephesians, and Philippians, and his beloved Timothy and Titus, about their being "in Christ Jesus" and about Jesus Christ being in them. One hundred and sixty-four times in his comparatively few Epistles this Apostle of the Gentiles used "in Christ Jesus" or its equivalent. What does that mean but that man is to live by the life of God — man "lives to God in Jesus Christ" or man does not live. So you see what Bethlehem's *Madonna* means to you and me, and what the Incarnation means to all mankind.

To get a true concept of man you have to enter the Mind of God — and that is among the easiest things in the world to do; for, let expert exegetes with their modern approach make what they will of the creation story in Genesis; let them do what they like with the phrase "the slime of the earth" and with the "breath of life"; let them write learned tomes if they please on that "rib" of Adam's that God "filled with flesh"; let them fill whole libraries with their erudition, they will never cloud the Mind of God concerning man so long as we have the Prologue to St. John's Gospel and the Epistles of Paul. For all anyone needs to do to get insight into God's Mind is to read the opening verses of Paul's Epistle to the Ephesians. There he will learn that "before the foundation of the world," God had "chosen men out in Christ" and had "predestined" them to become "through Jesus Christ his adopted children." That is not only God's Mind; that is also His Will as Paul made it known to you calling it the "mystery of his will," which was, is, and ever will be, "to gather all creation both in heaven and on earth under one head, Christ."

Looking at Bethlehem's *Madonna* we see in her arms that "Mystery" Paul proclaimed. Jesus Christ is that "Mystery"; and he solves the mystery we have been stating and restating, namely, that men must become divine. As staggering as the statement might seem, it is the Truth of God who revealed it directly and indirectly, explicitly and implicitly, again and again in the Gospels, Epistles, and Acts; who revealed it in the Old Testament in shadow and symbol, in type and prophecy. The statement is true with the Truth of God's own Son who was Himself "The Truth." When telling Nicodemus what man's destiny was He said: "unless a man be born again . . ." This time we had to be "born of God." But that would have been impossible without Jesus Christ. His coming to earth as Man was most certainly the best possible "good news" for men! For it is obvious that since what is born of man is man, what is born of God must be divine. So it is "in Christ Jesus" that man becomes man by becoming more than man.

Now you can understand how literal Paul was being when he wrote to his Corinthians and told them that "if any man is in Christ, he is a *new creation;* the old state of things has gone; wonderful to tell, it has been made over, *absolutely new"* (2 Cor 5:17). It was almost belaboring the obvious, then, when he wrote to the Galatians: "What really counts is not circumcision or its absence, but being a *new* creature" (Gal 6:15).

Paul is the one who tells us just how we become the "new creation" and how we are to live as that "new creature." He has it all very pointedly in a few sentences: "Do you not know," he asks, "that all of us who have been baptised into union with Jesus Christ have been baptised into union with his death? Yes, we were buried with him in death by means of Baptism, in order that, just as Christ was raised from the dead by the glorious power of the Father, so we may also *conduct ourselves by a new principle* of life . . . if we have died with Christ, we believe we shall also live with him, since we know that Christ, having risen from the dead, will die no more; death shall no longer have dominion over him. The death that he died was a death to sin once for all, but the life that he lives is a life for God. Thus you too must consider yourselves dead to sin, but alive to God in Christ Jesus" (Rom 6:3–11).

All that is to be taken literally. There has been a "new creation." You have been made a "new creature." By Baptism you were given a "new principle of life." You were born again and this time you were "born of God" — and thus you became fully man by becoming more than man. All this, thanks to the Child in Mary's arms at Bethlehem.

The purpose of having you look at these two *Madonnas* has been to bring to as sharp a focus as possible your whole being and your entire life. You are a child of the Eve who first sinned, as well as of the "Second Eve" who was ever sinless. Hence you will become more and more like Cain, or you will become more and more like Christ. That is the challenge and the choice of life: either you become a murderer of your fellowman, or you become his savior.

Now you can see what is meant when it is said that we are all "spiritual schizoids." We are all carrying around a "split personality"; for we live ever with the "old man" and the "new man" within us.

Paul said that in Baptism we "put off the old man," and insisted that we had "been clothed in the new." We know Paul would not deceive. We are positive that he states truth. And yet . . . yes, even years, and many years, after Baptism we find that we have not "put off the old man" — nor have we been fully "clothed in the new." Did the Sacrament fail to produce its effects? Did something go wrong back there at the very beginning of this "new creation"? What is the meaning of this mystery? — *Solvitur ambulando,* as the ancients might say. Solve this mystery by living it! Paul said you did "put off the old and put on the new," but that was only the beginning. That was the gift of life. Now you have to live life! You "put off" Cain, as it were — but you have to keep on putting him off. You "put on Christ" — but life is not life unless you keep putting Him on more and more day after day.

It is normal for things to express themselves according to their natures. Bees should act like bees. Irrational animals like irrational animals. But man, to act like man, must act like God. The "new nature" received in Baptism should be made manifest by actions corresponding to that nature. In short, Christians should act like Christ. That is a life's work. Hence the effects of Baptism will be made manifest by your actions all your life. That is, you should ever and always be living according to that "new principle of life." God did His part at Baptism — and made you a "new creature." You must do your part — by becoming all that He made you.

Look at Paul's description of Baptism again and see that it is a Sacrament that immerses us in the mystery of Christ's Passion, Death, and Resurrection. Hence, if we are to live according to the nature given us in this Sacrament, we must be ready to experience the fullness of the mystery and know something of a personal passion, death, and resurrection. That means that we, by our labors and fatigues, our sufferings, sweat, and tears, our agonies of mind, heart, body, and soul, along with all the thrilling joys that come our way as we struggle to "put on the new man," must realize ever more clearly that we are thus plunging ever more deeply into that Mystery who is Christ, and thus becoming the kind of human beings God meant us to be.

Let us look at Paul's description once again and note that he tells us there were four happenings in our Baptism: we died, were buried, rose again, and returned to light. These four things are to remain true forever — and at the same time should be a continuing process.

First there was a death — a death to sin. Christ conquered sin completely. In causing us to die with Him in Baptism, He gives us a share in His victory over sin. That fact brings you face to face with a real puzzle which we will solve even before you state it. This "mystical death" to sin, achieved in Baptism is not like physical death which is always so total and so final. Our death to sin which we underwent "in Christ Jesus" at Baptism is susceptible to "more or less." It is not enough to have undergone it once. We must "die daily" as St. Paul says. We must live out our Baptism. "You have died," says St. Paul, "and your life is hidden with Christ in God. . . . *Therefore,* put to death the passions that belong to earth: immorality, uncleanness, lust, evil desires, and avarice . . . rid yourselves of all these vices: anger and passionate outbursts, malice, abusive language, and foul-mouthed utterances. Do not lie to one another. Strip off the old self and put on the new, which is being progressively remolded after the image of its Creator and brought to deep knowledge . . . Christ is everything in each of us" (Col 3:3–11).

Quite a demand to impose on a "dead man," isn't it? But you see Paul's point — and mine. The ideal is to go on, in real life, growing according to the "new nature" given in Baptism. That means we become more and more dead to sin, and more and more alive to God — and all "in Christ Jesus" in whom we were incorporated at Baptism. "Since you have risen with Christ . . . seek the things that are above. . . . Set your mind on the things that are above, not on the things that are on the earth" (Col 3:1, 2).

Our "burial with Christ" follows the same pattern. For Paul, who had told his Galatians that "all of you who have come to Christ by baptism have clothed yourself with Christ" (Gal 3:27), is the same Paul who tells his Romans that they are to "put on the Lord Jesus Christ . . ." (Rom 13:14). Obviously, then, it is a continuing process.

The same is true about our issuing into the light at Baptism. Paul tells how it grows brighter and brighter: "all of us," he says, "are being transformed into his [the Lord's] very image from one degree of splendor to another" (2 Cor 3:18) and he prays for the Ephesians that God "enlighten the eyes of your mind with a deep knowledge of him, that you may understand of what nature is the hope to which he calls you" (Eph 1:18).

We must grow. It is consoling — and thrilling — to know that God "has blessed us with every manner of spiritual blessing," and that these "correspond to his choice of us in Christ before the foundation of the world." But when we go on to read the purpose of that choice: "that we should be holy and without blemish in his sight," we blush. We know we are not without blemish. Consequently, we know we are not truly "holy in his sight." Therefore, we realize that we are not all God chose us out to be. There is the fact. This chapter was written to show you what is behind that fact. You were Cain before you became Christ. The two women hold in their arms the full explanation of *you*.

But you should never become the slightest bit disheartened. So long as you have life within you, you need never despair of "putting on Him" with whom you were clothed at Baptism. You have every reason for confidence; for Paul was apodictic when he wrote: "For our sakes God made sin of him [Christ] who knew no sin, so that *in him* we might become God's holiness" (2 Cor 5:21).

Note well that Paul sets us shooting not at stars, but at what lies infinitely beyond the farthest star — God's holiness. Now lest you turn away from this one and only goal that is set for man, thinking it utterly impossible, look quickly at the relationship that was set up between you and the Three-Personed God when your head was still wet with Baptism's waters.

First, you were made a *son of God*. Adopted son, of course; but truly son nonetheless. Realize that between the fiction that is human legal adoption, and the sacramental fact which is divine adoption, there yawns a gap as wide as infinity. Good people can adopt children who are not their own, and give them their family name; but they can never give them their family "nature." They can grant them a share in the family fortune, but never in the family's blood. There is a very real limitation to every legal adoption. But not so with the divine adoption. God made us His children not by any extrinsic denomination or staid legal form, but by giving us a share in His very Nature. We have been more than dignified by this adoption; we have, as the ancients were fond of saying, been "deified" and "divinized." There was, literally, a "new creation" and we were made "new creatures."

Second, as soon as those waters wet our heads, a new set of relations with the Holy Spirit sprang into being. "Do you not know," asks St. Paul, "that you are God's temple, and that God's Spirit dwells in you? If anyone destroys God's temple, God will destroy him, for God's temple, which you yourselves are, is holy" (1 Cor 3:16, 17). A little later in the same letter: "Are you not aware that your body is the temple of the Holy Spirit? Him you have received from God! You are not your own masters. You have been bought, and at a price! So then, glorify God in your body" (1 Cor 6:19, 20).

This relationship gives you duties, it is true; for you are not to "grieve the Spirit" (Eph 4:20) or to "extinguish the Spirit" (1 Thes 5:19) and, above all, you are not to profane this Temple of the Holy Spirit. But this Indwelling gives you more than duties; it gives you Gifts that are truly glorious. You know their names, but do you know their natures? For instance, what is the Gift of Piety but the Holy Spirit leading you on to the perfecting of your relationship to the Father; the Holy Spirit teaching you how to cry *"Abba —* Father"; God Himself teaching you how to pronounce the name Jesus aright? It is said that the Holy Spirit dwells in you. But let that not lead you astray. It does not mean that the Holy Spirit simply inhabits the body, quietly dwells therein. He is alive within you — and alive with all the life of God; which means He is ever active. Pius XII said the Holy Spirit is the "soul of your soul." He is "the new Principle of life" — and that life is Divine Life.

Finally, Baptism gave you a new relationship to the Son. It made you His *member*. That word tells the whole story; the entire mystery. For it bespeaks a union so intimate that even the inspired writers of Sacred Scripture seemed to be feeling around for images to clarify the intimacy, and analogies to explain the union. They spoke of the pure union of man and wife, the vital union of branch and vine, and cohesion found in the human body. Tradition, thanks to the early Fathers of the Church, went further and told how members and Head form one mystic person — the Whole Christ. But it remained for Christ Himself to manifest the sublimity, the divinity, the mystery in all its profundity, when, at the Last Supper, He prayed that *we might be one* as He and the Father are one! Ponder that oneness and you will see you are caught up in that eternal embrace of the Holy Spirit, which is the personal love-union of the Eternal Father with the Eternal Son.

Related thus closely to God, we should never fear that we may not be able to take our dogmatic truths and make them dynamic; to live what we have learned; to become what God has made us to be. He has made us holy with His own Holiness. Now how do we become what we are? — "Thus," said St. Paul, "do we attain to perfect manhood, to the mature proportions that befit Christ's fullness . . . let us grow up in every respect in love and bring about union with Christ who is the head" (Eph 4:13–15).

"Let us grow up . . ." That is the exhortation that can discourage as well as stimulate; for that goal is truly in the "Heaven of Heavens." How can we ever attain it? How can we "grow up in every respect"?

Well, what other alternative is there? If we do not become Christ — mediators between God and men, saviors of our fellow-man for God — what will we become? The two *Madonnas* we have been looking at in this chapter should make us realize there is no other alternative. We are not going to become like Cain —

murderers, if not of our brothers, then most certainly of ourselves.

This simplification of the issue is not new, is not mine; but that of every man who really thinks on ultimates. Teilhard de Chardin writes: "But what an absurd thing life is, looked at superficially; so absurd that you feel yourself forced back on a stubborn desperate faith in the reality and the survival of the spirit. Otherwise — were there no such thing as spirit — we should have to be idiots not to call the whole human effort off."

Those are strong words. And to the unreflecting they may seem like very strange words to come from a Catholic priest. But to the thinking man they are recognized for what they are: words of wisdom. The "problem of the absurdity of life" is solved by Chardin who tells there is no absurdity; for when given the choice between suicide and adoration, we see we have no choice to make. It is made for us — by our nature and our supernature. Thus the disorders of our very disordered times can bring thinking men back to the only real order: that of eternity and God. Not Cain but Christ. . . .

This calls for faith. But without faith, as we have seen, men die. But what we have not as yet seen, is that faith itself can be dead. St. James points this out in that very lively second chapter of his Epistle which begins: "Of what good is it, my brothers, if a man says he has faith but has no corresponding deeds? . . . Faith, if it does not express itself in deeds, has no life in it. . . . Really, just as the body without the soul is lifeless, so also faith without deeds is lifeless" (Jac 2:14–26).

It is so clearly reasoned a passage that anyone reading it can readily understand how Martin Luther was completely nonplussed as to how to get around it; so he refuted it by refusing to consider it. He called it an "Epistle of straw." It is that — but it is the straw of the Manger, the straw that makes bricks and builds the Temple of God.

Our faith must be a living faith, a lived faith, a faith that is truly alive. That means that we must kindle within ourselves the "living flame of love." For faith can burn with hate. St. James tells us that "even the demons believe." The devils have faith, then; but they have no love. So if we will be the men God became Man to make us, our faith will flame with love, and that love light will give us vision enough to see Christ in ourselves and in all others — actually, in the members of the Church; potentially, in all others. That vision will enable us so to see our fellowmen that we will love them; and that is life as God will have us live it. Life means love; Christian life means the love of Christ radiating out from us to all.

Janet Stuart, an English Madame of the Sacred Heart, put this clearly: "It is the glory of Christianity to have so well schooled, so well regulated the heart of man, to have made that heart so virginal and so strong as to be capable of loving more, and better than ever, all that is lovable on earth — and at the same time capable of always loving it less than God. The glory of Christianity is to have worked this prodigy that a holiness so extraordinary, a perfection so superhuman, as we find in Christian saints, neither destroys nor fetters the pure affections of earth. The saints did not attain to love of God alone by stifling in their hearts all love for their fellow beings; but, on the contrary, they learned to love all mankind, in a certain sense, more than themselves, by first loving God above all."

That is precisely what living faith leads to. Anything short of that is not true Christianity. It is not living the Mystery of Christ — especially the Mystery of His Incarnation. That is the Mystery of Love laid before us in the warm, winsome flesh of a newly born Child. That same God who became a Baby needing a woman's devoted care, craving to be taken in her arms and to her heart, wants to be at home in your soul. Incarnation bespeaks your incorporation in His Mystical Body; it also bespeaks His longing to be "incarnated" in your flesh, to dwell in your soul, to permeate your whole person.

"Christ asks for a home in your soul," writes Caryll Houselander, "where He can be at rest with you; where He can talk easily with you; where you and He, alone together, can laugh and be silent and be delighted with one another." Every time you think of Bethlehem and its Madonna, you should think of this truth and open wide your heart so that Christ can be *at home* there with you. Every time you think of the Incarnation you should see it

not only as a profound and puzzling mystery, but also and especially as a prodigious manifestation of love — of God's love for
you personally! Consequently, whenever you think profoundly on
life, you will realize it can be compressed, with all its wonder and
mystery, all its challenges and thrills, all its demands for choice and
stand, into the one word *Christmas*. But you must realize, as you
do this, that Christmas is a compound word. It tells not only of
Christ, but also of His greatest action — Mass.

Too many celebrate Christmas as a day, seemingly to the utter
forgetfulness of the dogma it expresses; one might say all the
dogma it compresses! Too many celebrate the feast, forgetting the
fact; which, in all truth, is the one all-important Fact. Too many
commemorate Christ's birth in the past, forgetting the more
pertinent and personal birth of Christ in the present — His birth
*in you*. Too many think that Christmas refers only to Bethlehem
and the birth that took place there, failing to realize that the second
syllable in this compound word tells much more of Christ's death
than it does of His birth, and then goes on to tell of His Resurrection, Ascension, and Enthronement at the right hand of the
Father. *Christmas* says all that; for it is a word which tells you
that Christ was born to offer *Mass*. It also tells you all that is
essential in the life story of any and every Christian; for it clearly
states that each was reborn "in and through Christ" that "with
Christ" *they* might offer Mass.

This compound word, which falls so easily from all lips, tells the
whole story of God and man: the Divine Romance that has been
going on since before God first said "Fiat" for Creation; and will
go on until the same Lover says "Finis" for the stoppage of time.
Christmas is a word that ties in a unity the birth and death of
Christ — and implies the unity of the same realities regarding
Christians; but it goes even further. There is an eternality to
Christ's Mass; for the Victim of Calvary rose from the dead,
ascended into Heaven, to be enthroned there for all eternity.
What happened to Christ in His Mass is to happen to each
Christian in theirs. That is the Divine Romance — and that is its
happy ending. But before that happy ending is reached, the lovers
— that is to say, the humans who are so beloved by God — must

learn just what love really is. That means they must follow Christ from Nazareth and Bethlehem all the way — even to Golgotha and then to Heaven. Love is a mystery. Life is love. That is why your life is replete with mysteries. But they are being solved by the insoluble mysteries of Christ's life. In His life, as in yours, Christmas leads on to the Presentation in the Temple.

# CHAPTER SIX

# The Mystery of Your Name

~~~~~~~~~~~~~~~~~~~~~~~~~~~~~~~~~~~~~~~~~~~~~~~

*"What's in a Name?"*

AFTER Gilbert Keith Chesterton was baptized into the Catholic Church he wrote: "My name is Lazarus, and I live!" Chesterton knew that Baptism was both a death and a resurrection. It buried him and brought him forth alive. He also knew that it was Christ who called him back to life, just as it had been Christ who called the brother of Martha and Mary out of the grave where he had lain for four days. "My name is Lazarus, and I live."

But after you have read St. Paul's lines to his Romans about this same mystery-filled Sacrament, you realize that Chesterton, right as he was about his coming back to life, was not perfectly exact about the name that comes to one who is called forth from the "tomb" of this Sacrament. For Paul, after telling of the death we die, and the burial we undergo "with Christ" in Baptism, spoke of our coming to life and having in us "a new principle of life." Then he specifies, saying: "If we have died with Christ, we believe we shall also live with him" (Rom 6:8). So Baptism is not a resuscitation such as Lazarus knew, but a veritable resurrection such as Christ experienced. We did not come back to our old life, but were given "a new principle of life" — Hence, instead of saying: "My name is Lazarus, and I live!" we can be more theologically exact and borrow from the Apocalypse and say: "I was dead, but how wonderful, I live forever and ever" (Ap 1:18).

St. John reports those words as coming from the lips of the Son of Man whom he saw standing amid the seven golden lampstands "clothed in a long robe and girded around the breast with a golden cincture. The hair of his head was white as snow-white wool; his eyes were like a flame of fire; his feet were like burnished bronze smelted in a furnace; his voice was like the sound of many waters." You know this Man of white-gold beauty, with the voice alive with the music of many waters. It is the Christ, and His opening words are typical: "Do not be afraid." How often those words have fallen from those lips! And yet we men will cringe in fear. How long will it be before we will learn?

John tells us how he fell down as if dead when he first saw this vision of beauty. But the right hand of this Son of Man rested on John and in words alive with all the joy of laughing waters He said: "Do not be afraid, I am the First and the Last and the living One. I was dead, but how wonderful, I live forever and ever, and have the keys of death and of the nether world" (Ap 1:12–18).

Dare you appropriate such language to yourself — just because you have been baptized? You dare not call yourself "the First and the Last" — such a title belongs only to the One Eternal, God. But as for the rest, you most certainly may dare, and, in point of fact, you must appropriate those words to yourself. For you were dead — and now, how wonderful! you live forever. You were dead by reason of that original sin you inherited from your First Parents. But, thanks to your "Eldest Brother," Jesus Christ, you came to life — and will now live forever. St. Augustine was very fond of saying that we were "made Christ" by our rebirth of those sacred waters and the Holy Spirit, but to explain yourself more clearly to yourself, we are going to insist that by Baptism you were made *Jesus Christ*.

Do you ask what is the difference? If so, the reply will lead you into a review of the wonders God has wrought in you. Christ means *anointed*. If you were baptized as an infant, you have no recollection of having been anointed during this Sacrament. Even among those who were reborn in their adult years it is exceptional to meet one who clearly remembers having been anointed. But each and every one of us who were incorporated into Christ by this Sacrament of initiation was anointed. We have accustomed ourselves to associate this word "anointing" almost exclusively with what is today called the Sacrament of the Sick, but which was formerly more widely known as Extreme Unction. There are "anointings" in each of the Sacraments that imprint a "character" on the soul. You were anointed at Baptism, and again at Confirmation. I was anointed a third time at my ordination. Chrism — which has the identical root as the name Christ — was used on you and me to mark us as belonging to Him who was "anointed" in the womb of His Mother and thus made *Christ*.

Anointings with oil are common in such ceremonies as the making of a king — and never forget that Christ is the King of kings — and you are His member. But anointings with oil are even more common in the making of priests — and never forget that Christ is the one Priest of the New Law — and you are His member. So the anointing you received at Baptism marked you out as of the royal blood of God — and set you apart as a priest. Baptism has been called "the ordination of the laity" from earliest times — and the laity in our times are becoming more and more conscious of their "priesthood." The word is in quotation marks simply to differentiate it from the priesthood of the ordained ministers of God; not to deny any reality to your share in the priesthood of Christ. No, you are His member, and He is Priest of the Most High God. It is inescapable, then, that you share in His prerogative of Priesthood. So in calling you and the Son of God Incarnate, *Christ,* I am speaking of your priesthood primarily — your kingship after that.

In passing, it may be well to state that the character imprinted on our souls by these three Sacraments in which there is a special anointing, is the character of priest. St. Thomas teaches this unqualifiedly. Hence, whenever you hear "Christ" or "Christians" hereafter, you should hear overtones of priesthood accompanied by undertones that tell of sacrifice. For that is the prime purpose of the priesthood — to offer sacrifice to God.

Once you have fulfilled your function *per Ipsum, cum Ipso, et in Ipso* — "through Christ, with Christ, and in Christ"; once you have offered sacrifice to God as the only High Priest of the New Law taught you and told you to do, then you merit the name, as He Himself merited the Name — of *Jesus*.

There is the difference between the two names: Christ means *priest* — or "one anointed to function as a priest"; Jesus means the Sacrifice the priest has offered to God has been accepted by Him, and the men, for whom the Sacrifice was offered by this priest, are saved. Jesus means *Savior*. Your name, received in Baptism and through Baptism, is *Jesus Christ*. You were made Christ by the Sacrament; you'll become Jesus by the Sacrifice. What's in a name? — Everything! Especially when that name is your name: *Jesus Christ!* "But to as many as welcomed him he gave the power to become children of God — those who believe in his name . . ." (Jn 1:12).

You "believe in His Name" — and with reason! That Name came from Heaven, brought to earth by an angel from God — not once only, but twice: the first time when he announced that Name to Mary; the second time when he addressed a young carpenter: "Joseph, son of David," said the angel, "do not scruple to take Mary, your wife, into your home. Her conception was wrought by the Holy Spirit. She will bear a son, and you are to name him Jesus; for he will *save his people from their sins*" (Mt 1:20, 21).

There is nothing left to doubt about the meaning of this Name. God would make its meaning unmistakably clear. With God, Jesus means one thing and one thing only: Savior. So it should mean to all men, especially to those men who have been made children of God and given this Name which is above all names. Your name, and my name, and the name of everyone baptized is *Jesus* — Hence, we have a work to do!

It would be more exact to say we have a life to live rather than a work to do; for it is only in the first form that people will see there can be no divorce between our religious life and living and what so many call their everyday lives. Never. We are not named Jesus only when we are in church or on our knees; we are Jesus twenty-four hours a day, fifty-two weeks a year, until time ends for us, and then for all eternity we will be Jesus as He is.

We are so reserved about the use of this Holy Name that few of us recognize the Name as our very own. It was given us in our "resurrection from the dead" and our being made a "new creature" by the grace of the Sacrament of Baptism." Our name is Jesus. Since names signify natures and natures manifest themselves in their specific actions, our life's work, and the work of all our living is obvious: we must be saviors.

What's in a name? — In this Name St. Bernard of Clairvaux found Light and Food and Medicine. "Whence came there into the whole world so bright and sudden a light except from the preaching of the Name of Jesus," said St. Bernard. And you can well ask where is the historian who will not admit that the preaching of the Name changed the entire world, dissipating much of the darkness of ignorance, actually shattering the darkness of slavery, routing the darkness of barbarism, and flooding the world with the light we call civilization. What happened back there in the Dark Ages can happen in our Age of Blackout; for Christ still is, and ever will be, the Light of the world. We are His members — with a work to do. We are flames — or at least tiny sparks — in that Light. Jesus is your name and mine — and Jesus means Light.

The Abbot of Clairvaux said the Name of Jesus was *Food*. The Food that gives, nourishes, sustains Eternal Life — Jesus. St. Bernard asserted — and he was speaking from experience — that nothing can more fittingly or fully feed the mind than meditation on the Name of names — Jesus. Having been made acquainted with what is called "brainwashing," we know what food can do to the mind. The analogy with the body is perfect: Poison food will poison. Perfect food will perfect. And that Jesus is the Food *par excellence* no one who has tasted will deny. Bernard said it is a Food that will restore energy to any and every faculty that is weary, give strength to every good habit, more vigor to any and every virtue, and above all it will invigorate charity — or love. Could anyone prescribe more adroitly for our hungry, thirsty, poison-minded world? Bernard claims Jesus is "honey to the mouth, music to the ear, gladness to the heart." We can go further and insist that it is wine for the whole man — and it does what Scripture promised good wine would always do: it lifts the mind, heart, and whole man high up in joy. Does our sick world need joy?

That brings us to Bernard's next point: This Name of Jesus is *Medicine*. "Is any among you sad?" asked the saintly Abbot of his monks. "Let Jesus come into his heart, and his mouth echo His Name, saying: 'Jesus' — and lo! the light of that Name disperses every cloud and brings sunshine back again."

That sounds like a large promise. But if you doubt it — try it! *Solvitur ambulando*. Repeat that Holy Name with reverential *realization of all it means;* repeat it with heart and head attuned to the personal resonances it holds for you; repeat it with acute consciousness that because it is His Name it is also yours. Then you will experience all that Bernard promised to his monks — and more. For while Bernard was able to take his monks into his confidence and say to them: "Let us see how all this comes to pass . . ." and then go on to explain to them, you, with your present-day knowledge of, and your present-day consciousness of the living truth of the Mystical Body, can give an even more realistic and revealing explanation.

Bernard said: "When I pronounce this Name of Jesus, I bring before my mind the Man, who by excellence is meek and humble of heart, sober, chaste, just, merciful, and filled with everything that is good and holy, nay, who is very God Almighty — whose example heals me, and whose assistance strengthens me. I say all this when I say *Jesus*. Here I have my Model; for He is a Man — and here I have my Help; for He is God" (*Sermon XV on the Canticle*).

You can say more. For Jesus is more than Model to you; He is your Head. You are His member. Jesus gives you more than help; He gives you life — a share in His very own Divine Life. He makes you partake of His Nature. And all this for one definite purpose: to enable you to live up to your name — *Jesus* — and *be* a Savior.

In the past chapter you saw how Jesus lived up to His Name — by offering Mass. You will live up to your name no other way. You must offer Mass. For this were you born. . . .

When Christ had said to Pilate: "My Kingdom is not of an earthly character," the Roman governor snapped Him up with:

"Then you are a king after all!" The Prisoner then utters the line which is charged with more divinity than even that reply He had given the Sanhedrin the night before when the high priest exclaimed: "Therefore, you are the Son of God." To them Jesus simply said: "I am as you say." But to Pilate He gives a lengthier, and, it seems, a weightier reply: "You are right, I am a king. For this purpose was I born, and for this purpose I came into the world — to give testimony to the truth" (Jn 18:37).

In those words: "For this purpose was I born . . ." eternity rings. And in their resounding repetition: "and for this purpose I came into the world . . ." is clearly heard the decree of the timeless God. The thunder of divinity and eternity reverberates in that hall as this quiet Prisoner calmly, deliberately, majestically instructs His judge. Christ was saying that He was born to live up to His Name; that he had come to earth to be *Jesus* — Savior. As Christ spoke these simple words, so charged with mystery and divinity, we must realize He was moving on in His Mass. Then it will come home to you that you, too, must move on in your Mass; for it is as true of you as it was of Christ: "for this purpose were you born . . . for this purpose have you come into the world": to offer Mass "in Christ."

There again is recalled for you that word which holds within itself the entire mystery of Christianity: *Christ-Mass;* for it was by offering Mass that Christ became *Jesus* — lived up to His Name by "saving his people from their sins."

What's in a name? — What's in the name given you at Baptism: Jesus Christ? — The confident, cheerful, and, to the unbeliever, the always disconcerting reply to life's most persistent question: *Why?* Because our name is Jesus Christ we answer all life's *Why's* with *"Why not?"*

The explanation of that attitude of soul is enlightening and refreshing. At Baptism you reenacted in your life the mystery Christ enacted when He was presented in the temple. It is part of the baptismal ceremony to bring you into the temple of God — the Church. And that ceremony is saturated with symbolism, which should flood your world with joy. No matter where you happened

to have been baptized, the fact is that in and by that Sacrament
you had your "presentation" just as Christ had His when He was
but forty days old . . . and for the identical purpose!

You know the story. Forty days after His Birth, Mary and
Joseph carried Him to the Temple. It was the law. Mary had to be
purified, and Jesus presented to God. But what a mystery that
faces us with! How can immaculateness be purified? How can spot-
lessness be made clean? How could this law ever be applied to
Mary? — Yet, to the Temple she went — and to be purified! She
came also to fulfill the law which said "every firstborn male is to
be consecrated to the Lord." Look at St. John's Prologue. Read
how "when time began the Word was there, and the Word was
face to face with God, and the Word was God. This Word, when
time began, was face to face with God" (Jn 1:1–2). Yet Mary
and Joseph now carry this Word into the Temple "in order to
present Him to the Lord." This mystery raises questions, doesn't it?
But let us preface every rising question with the truth that this is
God — "who can neither deceive nor be deceived" — who is being
"presented," and His Immaculate Mother who is being "purified."
Obviously there is more here than meets the eye. What is this
all about?

Before you answer that last question, hear Simeon as he takes
the Child into his aged arms: "Now you may release your bonds-
man, O Master, according to your promise, in peace! For my eyes
have looked upon the *salvation* which you have prepared for all
the nations to behold, a Light to illumine the Gentiles, a Glory to
grace your people Israel" (Lk 2:28–32).

Luke tells us "His father and his mother were wrapt in wonder
at what was being said about him" (Lk 2:33). Maybe it will help
you realize that what Simeon exclaimed about Christ then, can be
said about you now! I have italicized the word "salvation"; for that
is the operative word. You are involved in what has been aptly
called "Salvation History." Conscious as you are of God and His
sovereignty, you can very well turn those words around and call it
"His Story of Salvation" — for that, to the theological mind, is
precisely what History is. Simeon's words tell you that you are to
do what Jesus did — live up to your Name of Savior.

Christ was carried into the Temple to be *offered* — to God. Again we face the meaningful word: *Christ-Mass*. Mary, holding out the Child in this ceremony of Presentation, was holding out, in the paten of her hands, the Body and Blood of Him who daily comes into our chalices under the guise of wine, and under the appearances of bread into our Hosts. She was priestess that day, if ever. For she was actually holding Him up to God who, on the night of His Last Supper, would hold Himself out and say: "This is my Body which shall be given for you. . . . This is my Blood which shall be shed for you. . . ." In Him, at the moment of Presentation, Mary was holding you up to God mystically — and offering Him your body and your blood for Christ's work of salvation.

There is the fact that explains much that seems inexplicable: you were presented in the Temple — to God — as an Offering! That makes life what God meant it to be: a Divine Romance — with Him the Lover, and mankind, each of us, the beloved.

Too many humans, either ignorant of their "divinity" or forgetful that God is Love, look upon life on earth as what they call "a battle of existence." They will wearily speak of "going on" in life. You must never miss what they are missing — you who have been lifted into the universe of the Divine. You are a collaborator with God. You actually play a part — and it is far from that of being a mere supernumerary — in Salvation History, which, in all truth, is a Divine Romance: the story of how God woos men back to Paradise.

Get the leading characters and the outline of the plot clearly. God created the world for Christ. That is Divine Revelation: "All things came into being through him [the Word] and without him there came to be not one thing that has come to be" (Jn 1:3). St. Paul has told you this again and again, but never more explicitly than when he told you that the "mystery of the will of God would be put into effect in Christ . . . since it was God's good pleasure to gather all creation under Christ" (Eph 1:4–10).

In Christ Jesus, then, the world acquires its meaning, its stability, its finality. In Christ Jesus the true dialectic of all history is to be found — and in no one else. In Him lies all our Philosophy

— or better, all our Theology of Creation, Time, Man, and Eternity. In Christ Jesus, and in Him alone, is meaning!

By now you realize it can be said that in you, Christ wants to "live and move, and have His Being." That is why you were born — in the waters of Baptism. That is why you came into the world — of God. That is precisely why you were "presented in the Temple."

If we were more Semitic, and less Greek, life would be different. For the Semites lived truth. The Greeks learned truth. We know we are creatures of God — even His adopted children. But, too often, we know those marvels only with a "notional" assent. Whenever the Jews gave an assent, it was a "real" assent. They translated the truth they had learned into everyday living and made it their very lives. We know that ontologically and theologically we are objects of God's thought and concerns of His Heart. But how often do we look upon ourselves as "thoughts" that God goes on thinking? His creative Mind (which includes His Will) is the source of our being, and the very center of our substance. But, with God, there are no "idle thoughts." He thought us, and keeps on thinking us, for the sake of His only Son. You and I are, because Jesus Christ was, and is.

Why was Christ? Why is Christ today? The one word "Christmas" tells you why. This Presentation in the Temple can tell you the same thing. The Incarnation lies at the heart of God's creative action. The Word was made flesh to redeem all flesh. You know how He did it. Christ was born to suffer. Christ was born to die — and rise again. Christ was born to become Jesus. In other words, His one great work in life was to offer Mass. That meant blood and sweat and tears; that meant agony. That called for scourges, thorns, spikes, and a cross. The Word was made flesh not only to dwell among us, but to have that Flesh hung on a cross.

All that horror was implicit in this Joyful Mystery of the Presentation. Something similar was implicit in your "presentation in the Temple" at Baptism — for you were then offered to God to prolong the Incarnation of His only Son. You were then made Christ that you might become Jesus. You were reborn that you might help change Redemption into Salvation — and thus bring the Divine Romance to its proper conclusion. In short you, like Christ, were born to offer Mass.

That does not mean that you were born to suffer. It means you were born to "rejoice in your sufferings and what is lacking to the sufferings of Christ supply in your flesh for the benefit of his body, which is the Church" (Col 1:24). Hence, this mystery in your life is joy-filling; for it tells you that your human existence has a divine purpose; that there is a transcendently profound meaning in every passing moment of time, be it filled to the full with pain, physical or psychological, agony of soul or body. It tells you that though your every day and every night be supersaturated, as it were, with frustration, you are one who can never fail — so long as you live up to your name.

We are not saying that there is pleasure in pain. This is Christianity we are teaching, not sadism. What we are saying is that there is no real mystery in what is called the "mystery of evil," that there is no real problem in what is called the "problem of pain" for those who live out the wondrous mystery of the Presentation. Briefly, there is joy in suffering for all who would live up to their Name of Jesus. "He [Christ], in view of the joy offered him, underwent crucifixion . . ." (Heb 12:2).

The Presentation in the Temple was a Joyful Mystery for Mary, for Joseph, for Jesus. It was a joy-filling experience for Simeon and Anna. And it set all Heaven rejoicing. For this was the beginning of the end; this was the "Offertory" of Christ's Mass. It was joy-filled despite what Simeon said to Mary: "Alas! This babe is destined to be the downfall no less than the restoration of many in Israel! His very name will provoke contradiction, and your own soul, also, shall be pierced by a sword" (Lk 2:34, 35).

To truth-loving realists there is nothing more unreal than baseless, pollyannalike optimism. Hence, this claim, that there is joy in a Presentation that promises agony and then goes on to claim that there is joy for all Christians in whatever pain comes into their lives, demands a base that is as solid as God and as firm and fixed as Eternity.

Since Christians are the realists of all realists, and the most optimistic of all optimists, that base must be — and actually is —

the base of Christianity. That base, is Christ. Better still, it is *Jesus!* Because Jesus Christ was presented to God and accepted by Him, every moment in any man's life can be charged with the glory of God; for that life can be made sacramental, sacrificial, and consequently salvific, simply by offering it "in Christ Jesus" and *as* Jesus Christ.

That last thought is essential for the realization of our dignity. St. Paul called us the *pleroma Christi*. Which means that we who by Baptism have been "presented in the Temple" actually "fill out" Jesus Christ — just as added healthy flesh fills out our own bodies. That is how close we are to God. We are actually *in Christ Jesus*. But let us never forget that He is Conqueror. Consequently — the conclusion is immediate — we Christians are unconquerable. We are men who can never fail — so long as we live up to our name and be all that Paul's phrase implies.

Realism will now help our optimism. We Christians see our fellowmen greviously afflicted with a variety of bodily ailments. We face those facts and say that, thanks to our "presentation in the Temple" and to the Name that was given us which is above all names, diseases are not evil in ultimate reality. We even go so far as to call them blessings.

We do not ignore the large number of mentally ill. We know of the children who are called "underprivileged" and "handicapped." But we are realists: we see them for what they are! We see all these people as at least potentially, if not actually, the *pleroma Christi*. Each of them has been brought into being by the Father for the furtherance of the work of the Son. That they may become Jesus Christ, He is ever ready to have His Spirit brood above the waters of Baptism. The Three-Personed God is concerned about each such person; for each is important to the Three Persons who are the one true God.

That is why we, in our realism, insist that in all God's wide world there is no such being as a "misfit," no such being as one truly "underprivileged," no one who is actually "handicapped." For those whom the materialists of the day called "underprivileged" we regard as actually overprivileged, the "handicapped" as the specially favored, the "misfits" as God's dearest. Hence, not pity, but reverence is what these different ones should call forth. For every single human, no matter what his physical or mental condition, is sacred with the sacredness of God: made so first by creation; then more so by re-creation; and finally most so by sanctification. Each has his place in that Body the Father is ever forming — the Mystical Body of His only Son, whose soul is God, the Holy Spirit.

For you personally this Presentation means joy; for it tells you that though frustration fills your days and nights, you need never fail so long as you live on earth. You cannot fail so long as you live "in Christ Jesus"; for His Sacrifice has not only been already offered, but accepted. Hence, He is Victor, and *in Him* you will always be the same.

You hear it day in and day out: "Why?" Why does this cruel sickness come into your life or that of your dear one? Why is this palpable injustice visited upon you or your family? Why do you garner such little fruit from all your noble efforts? Why do so few of your plans work out? The sun goes down before your day's work is done. Tides turn before you can cross the harbor's bar. Winters close about you before your harvests are in. "Why?"

Your best answer may well be "Why not?" You have been "presented in the Temple." You have been offered to God as a gift. You are to be used by Him as He sees fit and as He knows best. Loving parents want only what is good for their children, and try to give them only the things that are for their good. But human parents, at times, have neither the means nor the knowledge to give their children exactly what is needed. But God, your Father, your infinitely loving Father, who is not only omnipotent, but also omniscient, who is Wisdom itself as well as Love, is powerful enough to give you precisely what you need. If you believe with all your being that God *is* your Father, you will know with your whole being that everything and anything, sin alone excepted, that comes into your life *is* a blessing.

Now you, by your "presentation," were made the prolongation of Him who was "destined to be the downfall no less than the restoration of many in Israel." You, too, were given a Name which "will provoke contradiction"; but a Name which spells salvation.

And since you must "supply what is lacking to the sufferings of Christ," you have but one reply to the "Why" of suffering, and that is: "Why not?"

You can phrase your reply in two other ways, and it will be as true as the above. Since you have had so often the corpse of Abel brought to your mind as you have studied the mysteries in your life, you may truthfully reply to life's persistent "Why?" by saying to anything that comes to you in the way of suffering: "It is just." You have looked at Eve with her firstborn at her breast, as well as with her firstborn dead on her lap. Hence you have every reason to say: "It is just."

The Incarnation of God's only Son was a work of love, a work of mercy, a work of infinite condescension. But it was also a work of justice. Jesus Christ was the very Justice of God as Paul explicitly said: "Christ Jesus has become for us God-given wisdom, and justice" (1 Cor 1:30). And again. "For our sakes he made him [Christ] to be sin who knew nothing of sin, so that in him [Christ] we might become the justice of God" (2 Cor 5:21). God's justice demands that the scales balance. We were born in sin. We have sinned since. We are ever inclined to sin. Therefore, "in Christ Jesus" we must "become the justice of God." And since it is true that "unless blood is shed, there is no remission" (Heb 9:22), we know why sufferings come into our lives: God's justice — God's mercy — God's love.

Name any mental or physical disease to which the human is liable, and the true Christian will name them for what they are: God's justice, God's mercy, God's love.

Conscious of your solidarity in the two Adams, your reply to life's ubiquitous "Why?" can be either "It is just" or "It is a privilege." You can look upon life's pains, afflictions, constant thwartings with "Why not?" on your lips — and song in your heart; for God is using you for His highest purpose. You are "filling up what is wanting." You are being *Jesus.*

I stress realism and optimism as the marks of the true Catholic Christian, for there is a mental malaise over the contemporary world outside Christianity. Because of it, before one will now be accepted by the so-called intellectuals, he must reveal as vividly as human media will enable him the *anguish* of modern man, even his *nausea*. Human existence must be looked upon as tragedy. The poverty of present-day man, his utter hopelessness, and the plumbless depths of the abyss toward which he is falling must be presented in words that can set one writhing.

It is understandable when one realizes that these would-be profound thinkers are looking only on the surface of things; they see all the motion, but never the Mover nor the purpose of the movement. Many of the events of our century have had about them the odor of death: two world wars, atheistic dictatorships, concentration camps with crematories for living humans, obliteration bombing of unfortified cities and towns, mass murder of thousands of noncombatants, atom bombs, religious persecution that make Nero and Diocletian seem mild. Looking only at the surface, real despair is inescapable. But there is the depth of God below these surfaces. God is rewriting His love story — and, in our time, He has been writing straight on some very crooked lines. There is purpose, divinely wise purpose, beneath and behind every upheaval that has taken place. The true intellectual looks down into the depths of these happenings to discern therein God's justice, mercy, and love.

Your name is Jesus Christ. It signifies your nature. Actions should be in accord with the nature. Hence, if you will live up to your name and be what you are, you must become a savior of men whom Christ has already redeemed. You will do that if you will be busy always about "your Father's business."

# CHAPTER SEVEN

# You and Your Father's Mysterious Business

~~~~~~~~~~~~~~~~~~~~~~~~~~~~~~~~~~~~~~~~~~~~~~~

*"Did You Not Know. . . ?"*

IT IS inevitable that this study of the mysteries in your life has taken on the nature of a study of God's ways with those He loves the most; for you are closer to God's heart than you know, and God is closer to you than you will ever realize. Your deepest drive is for intimacy with God. How you are to direct that drive, and how God Himself dynamizes it, can be learned best by seeing just how He treats those near and dear to Him. But the most profound reason for the direction this study has taken is that you are Christ; and since you prolong His Incarnation, you will find the mysteries of His life in your own, if you are true to your name and your nature.

That being the case, it will profit you to take a quick glance at the man who was more intimately involved in the Incarnation of the Son of God than any other man — Joseph, the village carpenter. What ecstasy he must have felt when Mary, this perfect woman, was to be his wife! The acutely God-conscious will understand that there was even higher ecstasy for Joseph when he and his wife-to-be vowed their virginity to God. What a God-filled marriage this was going to be! But almost immediately the heart of this just man almost broke when he found his espoused wife pregnant. That "dark night" ended in a dream made bright by an angel's awe-inspiring explanation. But soon Caesar's edict set the young carpenter on the road to David's city with his wife whose time was so near. But what a welcome David's city had for this son of David: closed doors, no room for them at the inn.

Eight days later Joseph had the joy of giving the Son of God that Name above all names — Jesus. Thirty-two days later he took his wife and Child to the Temple.

All of us are puzzled from time to time when God sends something into our lives which is a real "low" after some "high," especially when the "low" looks like something incompatible with God. Learn from Joseph, who shortly after the Magi's visit was awakened from slumber by an angel and told: "Rise! Take with you the Child and his mother and flee into Egypt! Remain there until I give you further notice. Herod is on the point of searching for the Child in order to take his life" (Mt 2:13). Joseph could well have recalled that other dream in which the angel had told him he was to name the Child "Jesus; for he will save his people from their sins." He could well have wondered over the fact that this Savior of his people had now to flee from a petty tyrant. We have no record of such thoughts. Could it be that, by this silence, God is telling us that one of the fundamental lessons for life with Christ is that we are never to question the dispositions of Divine Providence?

If that be not the lesson then surely it is that life is undulant: sunshine will be followed by shadow — maybe by storms. There will be sorrows in the life of every Christian. But, as you learned from the Presentation, these can bring joy. In her *Hymns to the Church* Gertrud von le Fort has the line: "I will go into deepest sorrow that I may find my God." How strange that line sounds; but how profound is its theology! The poet means that it is not sorrow, sadness, or suffering that God sends us, but a gift that He grants in allowing us a special share in the work of His only Son. Thus it is that in what the worldling will look upon as heartbreaking sorrow (which, in point of fact it well may be!) you can find your God — and thus find Heaven.

The world shrinks from pain, runs from anything that may afflict body or mind. That may well be the full explanation of why so many fail to find Him who redeemed mankind by an Agony in His Mind and Body. The clearest solution to the problem of pain was given in that Flesh in which God dwelt among us, and in which He suffered such pain as no other flesh will ever know.

Pain presents no problem to those who know Jesus Christ. In fact, they recognize it not only as purposeful, but as a privilege God grants to His favorites. It is God's love. The Presentation proved this to you. The mystery in Christ's life and your own, which you are now about to study, will show you that God's love beats with a rhythm unmistakable. You are now to realize that there never would have been the joy of the finding in the Temple had it not been preceded by the loss of the Holy Child. Much of the mystery in your own life will be solved once you grasp the truth that the First Sorrow in our Lady's life ended as the fourth Joyful Mystery.

We are following the Gospel story of Jesus and Mary closely as we endeavor to solve the mysteries in our own lives because, just as there is no other truly "good news" than that given in the Gospel, so there is no other solution to the mysteries in our lives than that found in the mysteries of theirs. St. Paul makes this point sharply when he writes: "Our gospel is a mystery, yes, but only a mystery to those who are on the road to perdition, those whose unbelieving minds have been blinded by the god this world worships, so that the glorious gospel of Christ, God's image, cannot reach them with the rays of its illumination. . . . The same God who bade light shine out of darkness has kindled a light in our hearts, whose shining is to make known his glory as he has revealed it in the features of Jesus Christ" (2 Cor 4:3–6). To see yourself as you should be, look on the "features of Jesus Christ." That is what you have been doing since you first looked on the Corpse found at the opening of your story. Reread the familiar words of St. Luke: "Year after year his parents went to Jerusalem for the feast of the Passover. And so, too, when he was twelve years old they went up according to their custom at the time of the feast. After spending there the required number of days, they prepared to return, but the child Jesus remained behind at Jerusalem, without his parents knowing about it" (Lk 2:41–43).

The Son of God, true God of true God, who gave the Ten Commandments, the fourth of which is "Honor thy father and thy mother," is the same who as the Son of Man "remained behind at Jerusalem *without his parents knowing about it.*" An observant physician friend of mine remarked that a child of today acting as did the Christ Child in the long ago, would be called a "juvenile delinquent." That not only pinpoints the problem for us, it is the key to our solution. We know that, at the time, Jesus was but twelve years old — but we also know that Jesus was not a "delinquent." Yet here is an act that has all the earmarks of a delinquency. Herein could be *the* lesson God wants us to garner from this portion of the Gospel narrative.

For the time being we pass over the three days of agony of Mary and Joseph and focus our attention on the reply this Boy of twelve gave His bewildered Mother when she asked: "Child, why did you behave toward us in this way? Oh, our hearts were heavy — your father's and mine — as we searched for you!" You can all but see the look on Mary's face as she said this. You can almost hear the tone of her voice. But you could never prepare yourself for the reply she received. Luke tells us that Jesus' first words were: "How is it that you sought me?" What a question for a child to put to a mother who has been frantic for three days and three nights because she had lost him! But then Christ goes on with what, at first, is even more bewildering: "Did you not know that I must be about my Father's business?" She had just told Him that she and His father had been searching for Him with hearts that were heavy with sorrow. He tells her that He "was about His Father's business." No wonder Luke adds: "They did not grasp the meaning of his reply." How could they?

What Mary and Joseph did not understand then, you and I can understand now. Jesus was saying that earthly parents, at times, may have to suffer because of the demands of those other Parents of ours: God and His Church. He was telling every child by example what He would one day in words tell huge throngs; for it is the same evangelist, Luke, who records how "One day when great crowds were journeying along with him, he turned around and said to them: 'If anyone comes to follow me and does not hate his father and mother, his wife and children, his brothers and sisters, and even his life, he cannot be my disciple'" (Lk 14:25, 26).

Our God can be a very demanding God. The "good and gentle Jesus" can require things that are far from "gentle" and seemingly anything but "good." "Our Father's business" is one that commands as investment our entire being! In the Old Testament it was: "My son, give me thy heart" (Prv 23:26). That means life. In the New Testament it is even more explicit: "Anyone who does not hate his own life cannot be my disciple" (Lk 14:26). With our God there can be no half measures.

How dramatically Christ teaches our twentieth century! By seating Himself "among the rabbis, now listening to them, now asking them questions," while His virgin mother and His virgin father were seeking for Him with breaking hearts, He was teaching both parents and children of this present day that they must "be about their Father's business" — a business which may often tear them apart physically and emotionally. Sons and daughters may have to conduct this "business" far from their earthly father's home. There are such things as religious vocations which demand that children be lost to their parents not for three days and three nights, but for life. There are calls to the mission fields — calls that will demand that young men and young women be like Abram and "go forth out of thy country, and from thy kindred, and out of thy father's, and come into a land" which God will show them (Gn 12:1). At the age of twelve the Child Jesus is telling His own parents, and the parents of all time, that while it is proper for parental love to be possessive, it must never be overpossessive, for every child is first, and finally, a child of God. God alone may make total demand.

Is it not strange that we so often forget that we have been "born of God"; that we *are* His children, and He *is* our Father? It is astonishing that we forget, that we are acutely conscious of almost everything but the one thing that should crowd our every conscious moment: "the Father's business." God came to earth to teach us the way to Heaven. The first recorded words of this Son-of-God-made-Man are: "Did you not know that I must be about my Father's business?" Could a life directive be more clear?

At the age of twelve Jesus Christ teaches truth to those of all ages. He deliberately loses Himself in Jerusalem to underline the truth that the one business of life for you, for me, for every man is "the Father's business"; and that nothing whatsoever, nor anyone, no matter how dear, is to interfere with that "business."

God is a demanding God. But He is also a highly rewarding God. This same Jesus who, at the age of twelve, seemed so hard on His mother, and, consequently, hard on all who would be His disciples, is the same Jesus who at the age of thirty or more said to Peter and His other close followers: "I tell you with assurance; no one gives up home, or brothers, or sisters, or mother, or father, or children, or lands, for my sake and for the sake of the gospel, but receives a hundred times as much — now, in this world, homes and brothers and sisters and mothers and children and lands, along with persecutions, and, in the world to come, eternal life!" (Mk 10:29, 30.)

That shows that we are in a "business" that can never fail; one that brings high returns in this life, and in the life to come the return of all returns — bliss. But it is a "business" that requires our full attention.

This mystery in the life of Christ called "The Finding in the Temple" is one that tells us that although there is much in our Father's business that we will never understand, so long as we are truly intent upon our Father's business, there is nothing in the world that can really go wrong. There, in Jerusalem, Mary, we are explicitly told, "did not understand," yet she was wise enough to realize that, despite all appearances to the contrary, nothing was really amiss. We must be as wise, and though our world be turned upside down and inside out, so long as we are engaged in our Father's business we can say with Juliana of Norwich: "All is well! All is very well."

We know the end object of our Father's business: "to gather all creation . . . under one head — Christ." We have seen our part in the conduct of that business: we are the *pleroma Christi* — who are to "supply in our flesh what is lacking to the sufferings of Christ." We have rightly concluded that so long as we perform the duties of our state in life, precisely because those duties are God's Will for us, we are making every moment of time heavy with dividends for eternity, as we are hastening the second Coming of Christ. Such realizations, born of meditation on revelation, not only simplify life, dignify every human being, and charge every split second of time with the glory of God, they also challenge us at every split second to become what we are by growing up "in Christ Jesus" and as Jesus Christ. "Thus we attain to perfect manhood," says Paul, "to the mature proportions that befit Christ's fullness. Thus we shall no longer be children . . . let us grow up in every respect" (Eph 4:13–16). If we are not growing, we have reason to ask if we are truly living.

No one is exempt from the duty to "grow up" in Christ and as Christ; no one is exempt from the demand of God that they be holy.

Christ has shown us how we are to do all this. After being found in the Temple we read that he "advanced in wisdom and age and grace before God and men" (Lk 2:52). We must make the same "advance." But this mystery in Christ's life is showing us that our "advance" will never be in a steady, straight line. Life is undulant: made so by God, made more so by man. God will hide Himself at times, just as He hid Himself from Mary and Joseph for these three days. But more often it is we ourselves who try to hide from God; for we are kin to Cain, as well as to Christ, and have a mother named Eve, as well as one named Mary. In other words our human nature is still ours despite its very real share in the Divine. Hence, there will be detours, halts, and even backtrackings as we climb toward maturity in Christ. By prayer and penance, by the Sacrifice and the Sacraments, by works of mercy and of supererogation we steadily climb, making a *regular* ascent, even though not a straight ascent. Our life will be undulant, but it will also be steady growth.

We have insisted that "duty done spells sanctity." Consequently, our Father's business can be reduced to the duties of our particular state in life. But let it never be forgotten that the first duty in every state is God. "Like Father, like son" has perfect application in our case. We are sons of God. Our one work is *become what we are*. That is how we grow up; and that is really our contribution to the discharge of our Father's business.

St. Luke concludes his narration of this episode in the Temple by saying: "He went down in their company and came to Nazareth, where he was subject to them" (Lk 2:51). That one sentence sums up the next eighteen years in the life of God in the flesh,

just as this one episode is all we have of His early years after the
return from Egypt. In other words, we have one sentence from
the lips of God's only Son for thirty of the thirty-three years He
spent on earth — and that one sentence had to do with the
"Father's business"; second, all we know about His "hidden life"
is that He was subject to His parents and that He advanced in
wisdom, age, and grace.

That little knowledge coupled with that massive silence can
solve the mysteries in anyone's ordinary life. Christ was the Light
of the world. He called Himself such. The world into which He
came was dark indeed. Yet, for thirty years, this Light of the world
hid Himself. To have come to be the Light of the world and yet to
hide away from that world for ten-elevenths of a very short life;
to deliberately become a "Nobody" from a "Nowhere" while God's
people were crying for a Messiah; to go about life in the ordinary
way of the ordinary folk of the village while all the world was in
anguish for Redemption, would seem insanity if we did not know
it was the wisdom of God. We are His children who are to acquire
that kind of wisdom. The key to it lies in the word "ordinary."

That is an extraordinary word to use about God, but there is
no other when we wish to sum up His life and His doings for
thirty of His thirty-three years. When He returned to Nazareth
during His public life and taught one day in the Synagogue, "Most
of his hearers were puzzled," St. Mark tells us. "How did this man
learn all this?" they said. "The wisdom bestowed on this man —
what sort of thing is it?" and "His hands — what mighty works
they do!" — "Is not this man the carpenter, the son of Mary,
and brother to James and Joseph and Jude and Simon?" and "Are
not his sisters our nextdoor neighbors?" so, therefore, his person
was a puzzle to them (Mk 6:2–4). That can only mean that
Jesus lived among them in a very ordinary way, and passed for a
very ordinary man.

Yet, this "ordinariness" was highly pleasing to the Father, else
He would never have sundered the heavens at the Baptism of
Christ by John to say: "This is my Son, the beloved, with whom
I am well pleased" (Mt 3:17). Nor could Christ have made the
boast: "I do always the things that please the Father" (Jn 8:29).

Further, we must realize that Christ was always "about His Father's business." Hence, He was redeeming mankind doing those ordinary things down there in Nazareth as truly as He was when hanging on a cross outside Jerusalem. His every ordinary act, such as planing a board, hammering a nail, fashioning a plow or a yoke, even doing the ordinary things about the house, such as making His bed, sweeping the floor, washing the dishes, were actions of infinite worth, first, because He was an infinite Person; second, because those ordinary actions were the discharge of that extraordinary decree of God to save all men.

Now you are in position to draw proper conclusions. This mystery of the Finding in the Temple, coupled with the longer mystery of His hidden life, speak directly to you about your often mystifying and almost always very ordinary life. Christ teaches that there is no man, no matter how poorly endowed mentally, physically, socially, or financially, who cannot be more than man, and do greater things than the merely human; He teaches that there is no man, no matter how weak in body, mind, or soul, who cannot have the strength of omnipotence; that there is no man, no matter how simple of mind, who cannot act with infinite wisdom; finally, that there is no man, no matter what the meanness of his situation, as the world estimates meanness, who cannot bear in his being the beauty, the nobility, the majesty, the very divinity of the features of Christ.

There is no human being who does not burn with desire to do something worthwhile, something that will benefit his fellowman. That desire can be satisfied to the full by any and every man, no matter how endowed or unendowed he be, by being what he has been made to be by Christ — His member. For so long as one is "about his Father's business," no matter how hidden his life, and insignificant his deeds according to human estimates, he is actually doing a work that requires omnipotence; he is helping Christ please the Father by saving man. Christ redeemed mankind by doing His duty in the state of life God placed Him. We are Christ's prolongation. We will save mankind by doing as He did — by being obedient to the Will of God, found in the duties of our states of life. We are saviors. It is our duty to become what we are. We can do that only by living "in Christ Jesus."

If we live that way, our very ordinary lives will be resplendent with the glory of God. Pascal once wrote: "Great geniuses have their empire, their grandeur, their brilliance, their luster, their victory. They have no need for material splendor, for they live in a world apart. The saints have their empire, their brilliance, their luster, their victory, and have no need for earthly or intellectual grandeur; for their realm is something else" (*Pensées,* 793). He would have been more accurate, and he would have been describing you to the life, had he written: ". . . (their realm is) *Some-one* else."

Your "realm" is Christ. As Paul said: "your life is hidden with Christ in God" (Col 3:2). Christ had His "hidden life" — so do you have yours. In His, He was always "busy about the things that pertain to His Father" — always "doing the things that pleased Him" — and thus did He go about the "business" of redeeming men. There is your pattern for life and for all your living. It spells joy — not only for now, but forever.

# CHAPTER EIGHT

# This Mystery Puts You on the Way to Glory

~~~~~~~~~~~~~~~~~~~~~~~~~~~~~~~~~~~~~~~~~~~~~~~~

## *Not Your Relatives, but Your Relations!*

IN THIS probe into the mysteries in your life we have found your relatives so deeply implicated in the mysteries that make up your life and which shape your life's true story that everything that has happened to you can be traced back to them. You lead, have led, and will continue to lead the life that is yours because you were carried in the wombs of Eve and of Mary; because your elder brothers were Cain and Christ; because you who were born of Adam were also "born of God." These facts account not only for all your past and your present, but will account for all that will constitute your utterly endless future.

Yet the ultimate solution to the mysteries in your life lies not so much in your relatives as in your relations.

Heredity is a fact. From our human parents we inherited much of what makes us as we are. But the more important reality is that, from our other Father, we received much more than human parents could ever give. God, who is our Father, gave us a free will. By using that and His grace, we can become more and more what He made us to be when He granted us our second birth — re-creating us to a "newness of life" thanks to which we can be made more and more "conformed to the image of his Son" (Rom 8:29).

You were related to God before you were baptized, but once those waters had fallen on your head, a new relationship was brought into being which set you in a new orientation toward each of the Three Persons of the Trinity. It is a breathtaking truth, for the way you live out this new relationship will determine how, where, and with whom you will spend your eternity.

You know your relationship to the Father, for you have seen how "He chose you out in Christ before the foundation of the world." Further, you know your relationship to the Son who, though by nature the Only Begotten of the Father, became the "first-born of many brothers." Finally, you know something of your relationship to the Holy Spirit; for "because you are His son, God sent the Spirit of His Son into your heart, so that you can cry: 'Abba! Father!'"

Since it is "through Christ, with Christ, and in Christ" that you have become what you are: a son of God, it is obvious that the relation between you and the Father is a *filial* relation; for the grace — that participation in the Divine Life — which was given you at Baptism, was a filial grace, a filial participation in the Divine Nature. Do you sense the profundity of that relation? Filiation is one of the constitutive elements of the Blessed Trinity. How "like unto God" this Sacrament makes one! What the Son is by nature, you become by grace. As St. John insisted in his wonderful First Epistle: "We *are* children of God — not merely in name but in reality" (1 Jn 3:1, 2).

But, close as is your relationship to the Son, your relationship to the Holy Spirit is just as close. He is the soul of your soul; the vivifier; the life principle. As He animates the entire Mystical Body of Christ, He animates you, a member of that Body. Could He be any closer? To make this relationship more tangible, realize that your fleshy body is an actual Temple of that Holy Spirit. In that Temple the Holy Spirit prays in and through you; in it He endows you with gifts, brings you His beatitudes, works at your sanctification. Moreover, right here on earth and in ever passing time, He labors at the glorification of your soul by transforming it into the image of the glorified Christ, and prepares the glorification of your body, which is one day to be raised from the dead. Since you can be filled with the Holy Spirit, in all literalness your life should be a "spiritual life" . . . animated, dominated, and driven on by the Holy Spirit.

Since it was this Holy Spirit who brought Christ into flesh by

overshadowing the Virgin, since it was the same Spirit who led
Christ into the desert to begin His public life by conquering the
devil in his wily temptations, since it was the Spirit who, as St.
Paul intimates in his Epistle to the Hebrews, led Christ to His
Passion and His life-giving Death, we will now allow this same
Spirit to lead us "into deepest sorrow that we may find our God."
The Spirit will lead us into what is truly "deepest sorrow" as He
leads us into the Passion of Christ, but instead of saying only that
there we will find God, we will be even more explicit and say: "We
will go into deepest sorrow that we may find our Joy, our Life, our
Love, our Glory," knowing that in finding our God under all
these guises we are going to find our real selves.

At the outset we must realize that as we enter the Passion of
Christ we are setting ourselves on the way to glory. There is the
depth of the mystery and its very solution in a sentence. We have
already seen that Christianity — or life in Christ Jesus — spells
highest optimism and is the secret source of true joy. But that is
saying too little. Christianity means glory — not mere human
glory, nor transient earthly glory, but everlasting glory. Glory is the
end purpose of every Christian's life. We live to give glory; we die
to get glory!

If it is true that the depth of the Incarnation lies in the Son's
reparation of the Father's outraged glory, and that the width of this
mystery lies in the Redemption of mankind, then the height and
length of this stupendous condescension of God lies in the truth
that the Son of God took flesh that as Son of Man He might be
glorified for ages unending when He had enthroned human flesh at
the right hand of God, the all-pure spirit. Jesus Christ is seated in
glory right now, and "in Him," as St. Paul so mysteriously says,
we are already seated. Since Christ stated that He was "the Way,"
and since He entered into glory by walking the Way of the Cross,
you can see why this is the mystery that puts you on the Way
to Glory.

As Christ approaches "His hour" what contrasts are to be seen!

It is the first Palm Sunday of all time. Christ has ridden into
Jerusalem on the foal of an ass. The common people have set
the city ringing with their shouts of "Hosanna," filled the streets

with palm branches, and strewn the way over which the foal would walk with garments taken from their own backs. It was triumph; yet, not total. The Pharisees were beside themselves with envy and rage. "You see," they say to one another, "we are getting nowhere. Look, the whole world is running after him."

At this high point of triumph Jesus Himself shades in a sharp contrast. Some Greeks have asked to see the Son of God. When word of their inquiry is brought to Christ He breaks out with: "Come at last is the hour for the Son of Man to be glorified! I tell you the plain truth: unless the grain of wheat fall into the earth and die, it remains just one grain; but once it has died, it bears abundant fruit. He who holds his life dear destroys it; he who sets no store by his life in this world will preserve it for eternal life. Whoever would be in my personal service must follow me; and then, wherever I am, there, too, my servant will be. Whoever is in my personal service will be honored by the Father" (Jn 12:19–26).

There is your call, and mine. There, too, is our promise of glory. We are in the personal service of Jesus Christ; for we are His members. His Father, then, will honor and glorify us, provided we be what we are.

But Christ did not stop that day with His reference to us. He spoke about Himself, too: "Now is my soul shaken in its inmost depths; and what shall I say? 'Father, save me from this ordeal?' No, no; for this very purpose I am facing this ordeal. Father, glorify your name" (Jn 12:27). Christ was talking about His Passion and Death. He begins by talking of His own glory, ends by speaking of His Father's glory, and has spoken of your glory and mine in between.

Not too many of us realize that the only time we find Christ singing — which is a sign of joy and love — is as He entered what was going to lead Him to His Death. It is in the Cenacle, at the Last Supper, where His Passion really began, that we find Jesus Christ in what looks like ecstatic joy. Read the record of that last night as given by St. John if you would read how Love poured out love to Love. Once Jesus Christ has assured His disciples that they had nothing to fear from the world, since He had overcome the world, He raised His eyes to Heaven and prayed in what seems ecstasy: "Father, the hour is come! Glorify your Son, that your Son may glorify you. . . . I have glorified you on earth. . . . And, now, for your part, Father, glorify me in your bosom with the glory I possessed in your bosom before the world existed" (Jn 17:1–5).

As Christ entered His Passion, then, His mind was filled with thoughts of glory. But as you read on in this magnificent seventeenth chapter of St. John you will learn that it was not only the Father's and His own glory He was thinking about, but the glory of His disciples who were present there then, and all the disciples who would follow him as history unfolded. "I am offering a prayer for them," said Jesus of His Apostles, "but I do not pray for them alone; I also pray for those who through their preaching will believe in me." The burden of His prayer is unbelievable! He prayed for oneness, but a oneness that is beyond our ken. "All are to be one," He said, "just as you, Father, are in me and I am in you, so they, too, are to be one in us. . . . The glory you have bestowed on me I have bestowed on them, that they may be one as we are one — I in them and you in me. . . . O, Father! I will that those whom you have entrusted to me shall be at my side where I am: I want them to behold my glory, the glory you bestowed on me because you loved me before the world was founded" (Jn 17:20–25).

That is God praying to, and pleading with, God — on your behalf and mine. His unbelievably bold plan for our unity and our glory with Him and the Father is based on His Passion and Death. How truly He loved us to death. How much more true that He loved us to life eternal! Our "Tremendous Lover" ends His prayer and plea for us with: "Just Father! . . . May the love with which you love me dwell in them as I dwell in them myself" (Jn 17:25, 26).

With such a revelation of love ringing in our ears and resounding in our hearts, we can plunge into our probe of His Passion confident that we shall find our God and our glory; confident, too, that we shall discover the solution to that problem which so many men consider insoluble — the problem of pain. We can be positive that we are about to unravel the mystery of suffering.

It is worthy of note that pain has not been a problem to all men, nor suffering a mystery to all minds. Some years ago Canon Sheehan calmly wrote: "The Mystery of suffering! The great eternal problem! And yet no problem at all if we only consider it as a Law of Being. . . . Is it not in the nature of things that suffering is inevitable?" He based his contention on three points: first, suffering is a necessary condition of imperfect beings; second, it is a necessary motive power in carrying on the work of existence; finally, it is an unconscious but most noble revelation to higher beings of facts and principles in the great economy of creation that perhaps otherwise would be hidden from them forever.

Sheehan admitted that such philosophical reasonings would never mitigate any pain, but he hoped that he might provide for others "a soothing thought that suffering is not the unreasoning and inconsiderate infliction on helpless beings of pain from the hands of a supreme and arbitrary power."

Recently another priest, Dr. Johannes Pinsk, wrote: "The determining characteristic of suffering — the thing that makes it what it is — is the sense of frustration, the realization of a threat to one's very existence. Suffering — be it corporal, or spiritual, or psychological in origin — always makes us painfully aware that we are on the ebb-tide of life. The final, the most bitter suffering of all, is death; but, at bottom, all suffering is but a foreboding of this ultimate dissolution. From this point of view, there is nothing mysterious about suffering. It is a necessary concomitant of life as we know it, and 'bitter' it is, without any qualification."

That is very good reasoning, but it would never lead one on to joyful endurance. Such philosophizing can at best generate a stoical attitude toward suffering. But once we go beyond unaided human reason, step from philosophy into revelation; once we have looked at Jesus Christ in His Passion and Death, all our thoughts about pain and suffering know a complete reversal of form. Philosophy would have us see in them the crushing misery of, and the maddening frustration in, earthly existence. But we know that no one in his right mind goes to misery singing; nor does anyone who is normal face frustration with ecstatic joy. Yet we have just looked on Jesus Christ at His Last Supper and found

Him in ecstatic joy and heard Him singing. So philosophy will yield place, and Mother Church will lead us by the hand into this mystery which ultimately spells glory.

It is rather startling to the superficial thinker to find the Church opening the Mass of Holy Thursday with the chant: *Nos autem gloriari oportet in cruce Domini nostri Jesus Christi* — "We ought to glory in the cross of Jesus Christ our Lord." Glory in the deathbed — and such a deathbed — of the One we love above all other loves? Glory in this outrageous affront to the God of majesty? Glory in this gibbet of shame? That is precisely what Mother Church tells us we ought to do. It would be positively shocking if she did not add the reason: *in quo est salus, vita, et resurrectio nostra* — "for in Him is our salvation, life, and resurrection"; *per quem salvati et liberati sumus* — "through whom we have been saved and made free."

No mourning in those lines. No lament. No expression of sympathy for the Lord God who underwent a Passion and died on that Cross. Just chants of joy — of what is close to exultation. That would be upsetting had we not the Gospels to teach us how we ought to view suffering — especially this torrent of suffering we call the Passion of our Lord Jesus Christ.

All the Evangelists, but especially St. John the Beloved, hurry over the Crucifixion. They report this fact of all the facts of history in a way no modern reporter would ever record it. Theirs is almost an impassive account. Nowhere will you read any high indignation over the way the priests, the Sanhedrin, Herod, Pilate, or the soldiers treated Christ. Nowhere is there any compassion or sorrow expressed. They do not minimize any of the pain. They detail all the brutality, the barbarity. All the anguish and agony are there. But it is expressed in so sober a fashion that any thoughtful reader is made keenly aware that underneath it all is some mammoth mystery. Christ, buffeted, beaten, bloody, unbelievably bruised, is always shown in full possession of Himself, always majestically calm.

It may have been Christ Himself who engendered in the Evangelists this cast of mind. For, whenever He spoke of His Passion — and He spoke of it often — He always added a word about His Resurrection. Matthew has one such account. The twelve with Christ are on their way up to Jerusalem. Jesus takes them aside for privacy's sake and says to them: "Listen! We are going up to Jerusalem, where the Son of Man will be betrayed to the high priests and Scribes, and they will condemn him to death, and hand him over to the Gentiles to mock and scourge and crucify" (Mt 20:17, 18). It is all there: the trials, the scourging, the mocking, and finally the crucifixion. But then Jesus added: "but on the third day he will rise again" (Mt 20:19).

True it is that in their accounts the Evangelists do not link the Resurrection explicitly to the Passion and Death; but in the Acts and the Epistles it is very noticeable that, while nothing is added about the outward events in the life of Christ, the inner meaning of the events, and especially of the Passion and Death, is laid bare. We are, then, given all the light we need to know the purpose of this dark mystery in the life of Christ, and thus are we given enough information to enable us to adjust to the similar mystery in our own lives.

God died on Calvary, but men came to life. "God brought you to life," says Paul, "with Jesus, when he forgave you all your sins, and cancelled the bond with its decrees that was against us. He did away with it when he nailed it to the cross. God disarmed the Principalities and Powers; he exposed them publicly to derision and displayed them in Christ's triumphant cortege" (Col 2:13–15).

A passage like that, telling that all this was triumph, enables you to understand the Church using such hymns in Passiontide as *Vexilla Regis* — a soldierly song that tells how "The Standard of the King advances, the mystery of the Cross shines forth. . . . Thou art beautiful and glorious, Tree decked with royal purple. . . . Happy art thou to have borne the World's Ransom suspended in thy arms." And again when she has us break out in accents of triumph and glory in the *Pange lingua* — "Exalt, O my tongue, the laurels of a glorious combat! Upon the trophies of the Cross proclaim the great triumph; Christ, the Redeemer of the World, comes forth as Victor from the combat in delivering Himself up to death."

There is the mystery of Christ — and the solution to all mysteries for Christians. The Son of God had to hang on the Cross because of our brother Cain. Mother Mary had to stand beneath that Cross because of our mother Eve. Human life had to be drained from God that we humans might have in our veins Blood Divine.

Small wonder that St. Paul summed it all up for himself — and for us — with his triumphant cry: "God forbid that I should glory except in the cross of our Lord Jesus Christ" (Gal 6:14). Small wonder that he added: "From now on let no man give me trouble, for I bear the marks of our Lord Jesus on my body" (Gal 6:18). That is what physical suffering can be, and should be, for you and me: "the marks of our Lord Jesus Christ on our bodies." That is what they will be if we now "go into deepest sorrow" and actually find God who is Joy and Glory.

*Glory* — How Paul stressed it! "Having, therefore, been sanctified by faith, let us have peace with God through our Lord Jesus Christ, through whom also we have found entrance into this state of grace in which we now abide, and exult in the hope of participating in God's glory. Not only this, but *we exult in tribulations* also, aware that tribulation produces endurance, and endurance proven virtue, and proven virtue hope. And this hope does not disappoint, because God's love is poured forth in our hearts by the Holy Spirit who has been given to us" (Rom 5:1–5).

That passage should be read and reread. For Paul has everything there. Faith that breeds hope — a hope that does not disappoint — because founded on, filled with, and to be fulfilled by love. Grace, that share in the life of God, leads us on to an expectation of a share in God's glory. How could we react otherwise when God's very love is poured into our hearts by the Holy Spirit who has been given to us? With all that before us, who would not "exult in tribulations"?

The secret of the joy in suffering is the personal discovery of the very strength of Christ within us with the consequent realization that, today, suffering is not so much struggling under the weight of the Cross, as standing in the radiant glory of the Risen Christ. That is the realization which changes what could have been in us, and on us, the "mark of Cain," into the "marks of our Lord Jesus on our bodies."

We go back to our earliest relatives so that you may realize again that all suffering is man-made inasmuch as, according to God's original plan, you were never to have known suffering, sadness, sickness, or death. Your original father and mother changed that original plan by what we call original sin. That sin was not only the origin of Cain's murder of Abel, but of every sin any child of Adam and Eve has committed since. That sin was also the source of all suffering, even of — and especially of — the sufferings we call the Passion of Christ.

With these relatives before our eyes, we can more surely appreciate the mercy and the marvel of the relation won for us by the Passion of Christ, and the change wrought in our attitudes toward suffering because we can live "in Christ." To know that suffering was the "mark of Cain," all we have to recall is the "mark" God put upon the first of all murderers. It was to brand him unmistakably as sinner. That would have also been our brand had not Christ died the Death and risen to glory. But after His triumph all suffering can be regarded as the "stigmata of Christ." That means that we live ever "Christ-conscious." Then we will do as Paul did and "rejoice in the sufferings we bear . . ." (Col 1:24).

But no man will ever be able to say that with sincerity unless he has first been able to say with the same Apostle: "I will boast of nothing save my infirmities. . . . Gladly will I boast of my infirmities, that the power of Christ may spread a sheltering cover over me. For this reason I take delight, for Christ's sake, in infirmities, in insults, in hardships, in persecutions, in distress. For when I am weak, then am I strong" (2 Cor 12:5–10).

It is really Christ in you who bears these sufferings. It will be you "in Christ" who will do the same if you sharpen your consciousness of being His member.

Suffering of any kind, let alone that of the Cross, will always be an absurdity to anyone who looks on it with only human eyes. Under such eyes even Jesus Christ in His saving Passion is naught but an object for pity — as He was to the weeping women of

Jerusalem that first Good Friday afternoon. But once we clear our vision by the use of the light of Faith, Christ in His Passion and utter misery is seen by us for what He is: "the power of God and the wisdom of God" (1 Cor 1:23).

With Paul we know full well that "there is more wisdom in the 'absurdity' of God than in all the 'wisdom' of men, and more might in the 'weakness' of God than in all the might of men" (1 Cor 1:25).

We will never know all there is to know about this mystery of the Passion and Death of Christ, but we most certainly know this: that it solves for us what is called the "mystery of suffering" and gives us the one answer to the "problem of pain."

With prayerful pondering we can move ever more deeply into Christ and His mysteries. That is why we now "go into deepest sorrow" with high expectations of meeting our God, who is our Joy and our Glory — and of also meeting our truest selves.

# CHAPTER NINE

# Four Mysteries in the One Word *Fiat*

~~~~~~~~~~~~~~~~~~~~~~~~~~~~~~~~~~~~~~~~

*On the Lips of the Trinity — Creation;*
*On the Lips of Mary — Incarnation;*
*On the Lips of Christ — Redemption;*
*On Our Lips — Salvation Through Sanctification.*

PAIN is "man-made"; it is not "of God." But, thanks to the God-Man, it can now be accepted as a priceless privilege, and used as a means to highest sanctity. Hence, the man of real wisdom, far from looking upon pain as an evil to be avoided at all costs, will recognize it as something to be accepted willingly and used as an aid in becoming what we are: collaborators with Christ in the sanctification and salvation of men.

Yet, it may be wise to insist upon a few other truths before looking deeply into this truth. First, Christianity is not a cult of suffering; it is a religion of joy — for it is a religion filled to the flowing over with well-foundationed optimism since it lifts man above himself, gives him a share in the life of God, and sets him on the Way to Glory. Second, Jesus Christ did not bring the cross into the world, nor suffering into human life. From the time Adam was expelled from Paradise to the time Christ was born at Bethlehem, the world had been steeped in suffering. By the time Christ was born the cross had been everywhere — and was both cruel and crushing. But because He bore His Cross willingly and submitted to His Passion joyously, because He was a Lover who loved both God and man "to the end," what before had crushed men, engendering only hopelessness and despair, can now lift man up to that nobility which is more than human, as it enables him to become what he is — "like unto God."

Pain and suffering are widespread, still cause tears to flow; but now, instead of being bitter, angry, and sterile tears, they can be like Cana's water: joy-giving wine.

Of course there will be those who will say sincerely that all this is most unreal and irrational. "Who can welcome suffering?" they will ask. "Who can embrace pain? Who can carry a real 'cross' with joyousness?" They will claim to be realists. There will be reasonableness to their stand. But against them stand the words of God!

As Christ sat down to His Last Supper His words were: "It has been my heart's desire to eat this paschal supper with you before I suffer" (Lk 22:15). Christ's whole being was longing to enter into His Passion. This same Evangelist tells how Jesus once said: "To throw a firebrand upon the earth, that is my mission. And, oh, how I wish it were already ablaze. But then, I have yet to undergo a baptism, and oh, in what agony I am until it is accomplished" (Lk 12:49, 50). Christ was the Realist of all realists. And there you have His attitude not only toward suffering, but toward agony.

Christ's close follower, St. Paul, was no man given to sentimental vaporings. Yet, when imprisoned in Rome, he sent out epistle after epistle, which cry out: "I am shackled. Yes, I am in prison. But, no! I am not in prison. I am in heaven. For I tell you I superabound in joy!"

What conclusion is left for us of the twentieth century to draw but that it is not Christ or His Apostle who is inflamed beyond reason in this matter of suffering, but it is we Christians who show a very real lack of reason by not being sufficiently inflamed?

Much space has been given in this book to the matter of suffering. And with reason. Life is undulant. Hence, there will be happiness as well as misery. But happiness never presents a problem. No one ever thinks of happiness as a mystery. Yet it is a profound one. In fact, since joy is the fruit of love, and since all love comes from God, and since God is the Mystery *par excellence,* joy can very well be called the mystery of mysteries. But it can also be said that joy presents no problem because, in a very true sense, it comes naturally to us. God made us for joy originally.

Had Adam not listened to Eve, we would never have known joy's opposite, nor ever be puzzled by what seems so contrary to our very nature.

Jesus Christ answered every possible objection to the prevalence of suffering in man's world, not by banishing physical pain or mental suffering from that world, but by undergoing both to the full and showing men how they can sublimate all suffering into *sacrifice* — and thus speak love's most eloquent language. Christ was human, but no humanitarian. He founded a Church that would pour out love — divine and human — upon all men, but would be no mere philanthropic organization. In that Church He established, as the center and source of all real life for men, His Holy Sacrifice, which shows, as nothing else could or can show, that if there ever was a fallacy in men's mind it is that which looks upon a sacrifice as something unpleasant. Christ showed that in real sacrifice there is a joy which surpasses all other joys; for in it total love is reached.

Too many, even among well-instructed Catholics, still think that every sacrifice must be painful; that we merit in proportion to the misery we experience; that somehow or other spiritual progress is measured by the increase in suffering. Nothing could be farther from the truth. God does not demand unhappiness as the price for happiness. He is no barterer who grants things only at a price. He is our Father — who gave us life without the asking — and created us for happiness not only in the hereafter, but most emphatically in the here.

Again and again we have to return to God's plan for us. We are immortal beings. God made us so by giving us a spiritual soul. Hence, according to His plan, what began at our conception is to go on everlastingly. What we call death is not an end to life, but only a break in the mode of living. The life of glory for which we men have been destined is but the full and final development of the life of grace which Christ merited for men by His Life, Passion, Death, Resurrection, and Ascension, and which is given to men in time. Analyze that truth and you will see that Heaven begins on earth; for, thanks to grace, we already live the life of glory in its seminal form. We already know and love God, and thus live the very life He lives. We already possess God. All that we lack of Heaven's bliss is that fuller light, called the Light of Glory, which will enable us to see God face to face.

The point is this: God is all-good, all-loving, all-powerful — and He is our Father. No one of those prerogatives can be questioned, especially since we have looked so long on that *Madonna* who was Mary with the Only-Begotten of the Father, a Child of her own body, in her arms, and on that *Pietà* who was that same Mary with the Corpse of that same Son across her knees. Since suffering is still an omnipresent reality on earth, it can only be concluded that suffering is not, cannot be, the real source of human unhappiness. If it were, God, to be true to Himself, would have banished it from earth long since — especially after His only Son had undergone so much of it.

But God is God — and Christ is His only Son, and our Way to the Father. Hence, what Christ did with suffering we are to do with it. The one word that will sum up all we have to do is the Latin word: *Fiat.*

That word can be translated as "acceptance," but it means *donation* as well as acceptance. It connotes a giving as well as a receiving. It signifies a donation of self to the will of another. That is what it meant for Mary at the Annunciation. That is what it meant for Jesus in His Agony in the Garden. That is what it is to mean to you throughout your life on earth.

One can go further and say that *Fiat* means creation. On the lips of the Trinity, at the beginning of all things, it meant just that. In addition to Creation, it means, Re-creation, Incarnation, Redemption, Salvation, Sanctification, and Glorification. On the lips of God it meant the first. On the lips of Mary it meant the second and the third. On the lips of Christ is signified the fourth and fifth. On your lips it will mean the sixth and the seventh — Sanctification and Glorification. And that, not only for yourself, but for many of your fellow humans.

Once we have learned to live *Fiat* we have learned the secret of happiness, of holiness, of genuine Christian joy. We have the key that unlocks mystery after mystery; we know what brought the universe into being, God into flesh, the God-Man back to the Father's side, and what can bring any man back home to Heaven. Right now our sincere *Fiat* will insure our sanity as well as our sanctity.

That last note is struck deliberately; for you, since you are human, are going to know mental anguish. In one form or another mental anguish is part of human life. But it means more than that to you. Since you are a Christian you are going to share in the mystery of the mental sufferings of Jesus Christ; for that is what it really means to be a Christian. Christian maturity is admirably defined as a loving understanding of the mysteries in Christ's life, and an intelligent, loving living-out of those same mysteries in one's own life. Consequently you are going to be your sane, saintly self, and show yourself a mature Christian only if you readily accept with a wholehearted *Fiat* everything that comes your way — especially mental anguish.

The note of sanity is being sounded again and again right here because your world is filled with mental anguish, but it is also far from being sane. One of the basic causes of its pitiable condition is its failure to accept utterly God's Will — to learn and live *Fiat*.

Many today are totally absorbed in the study of the abnormal, without once striving to establish a definite idea for what constitutes the normal. One can understand the difficulty so many of these men experience in endeavoring to define the normal man. But one cannot have too much patience with it. For the Gospels and the Epistles of St. Paul are open to the gaze of all men. In these, man, every man, has been given a very definite and utterly distinct Norm — and has been given such by God Himself. Actually that Norm was placed before the eyes of man the moment God found the first man guilty of sin; for this Norm was promised in Paradise. That promise was fulfilled when a Maid in Nazareth bowed her will to that of God and said, *"Fiat."* That Norm stood before us, "like to us in all things save sin," precisely so that we might measure up to that Norm and become "like unto Him in all things" — and especially in not sinning! *Jesus Christ is the Normal Man,* inasmuch as He is the Norm for all men. Of course He is not what we mean by an "ordinary" man; for He is the Perfect Man. But it is the Perfect Man to whom we imperfect men must measure up if we are to be all God wants us to be.

*Abnormality,* then, can be defined as *"departure from Christ, the Norm."* Departure from the sanity of the Son-of-God-made-Man is a mental disorder in any human. Departure from His sanctity will be a moral, or a spiritual disorder for any human. But realize right here, and thank God for the fact, that departure from the sanity of Christ need not be a departure from Christ's sanctity. Thanks to *Fiat* a mental disorder can be a means to high sanctity. But departure from Christ's sanctity is most assuredly a form of insanity; for every sin, in a very true sense, is insane — as insane as was that original sin, and every sinner is as insane as were Adam and Eve when they entertained the truly mad thought that by disobeying God they would become like unto Him.

The men of today need to be told these truths with force and clarity. For it would seem that Pius XII was something of a prophet when, in the middle of World War II, he said that the postwar man would be more changed than would be the postwar map. Though, in the physical sciences, postwar man is experiencing many triumphs which have given him ever greater mastery over this seemingly ever expanding universe; though, in the sciences of the psyche, he has made discovery after discovery, which should give him ever greater mastery over the tiny universe which is himself; and though such masteries should bring him a sense of security, integrity, and well-being, the opposite has eventuated. Never was man so unsure of himself, so fragmented, so insecure in his universe. Never has discouragement, disgust, and despair been so common. The *Angst* of Kierkegaard's philosophy is felt by too many moderns to be the very stuff of life. Consequently, Heidegger has millions echoing him by saying: *"Dasein ist Sorge."* — "Self-existence is worry." Anxiety plays too major a part in the lives of too many men, and has become too much of a commonplace on the lips of so-called modern philosophers. It is these latter who have given man his sense of frustration and utter futility; for the anxiety of these so-called philosophers is an anguish that has no issue.

It is these philosophies and psychologies that have been popularized in novels, movies, stage productions, and can be seen and heard almost hourly over radios and on TV screens. Man's susceptibilities being what they are, his suggestibility being what it is, there is no reason to wonder at the patent fact that the still infant science of psychiatry is inducing in many the very diseases it is supposed to cure when it does not prevent them. But it is not with mere anxieties, phobias, complexes and compulsions that we are now concerned. It is that deeper depth which present-day depth psychology does not, and cannot, reach; for it is in this deeper depth that postwar man has changed so much from prewar man. Yet, even this change can be charged, to some degree, to the popularizations of psychology and psychiatry.

It cannot be gainsaid that postwar man lacks an acute sense of sin. That, of course, can only mean that his consciousness of God has been badly blunted; for there can be no sin, if there be no God. Before modern man recovers his sense of sin, he will have to first rediscover his God.

Some few think it is the amazing triumphs achieved in the physical sciences that have produced in modern man his blindness to God and the consequent bluntness in his sense of sin. But it is more likely that the source of both blindness and bluntness lies in the sciences of the psyche. For these have produced in too many moderns the false belief that they are not fully responsible for their acts. Lessen liberty, and you lessen manhood. Lessen manhood in this way, and you lessen Godhood. Lessen manhood and Godhood, and what have you left in the moral universe? Depth psychology has taught much truth, but it has also engendered much error. It may not be entirely the fault of the sciences or the scientists. It may be due, ultimately, to man's proneness to look for any excuse to dodge responsibility, and free himself from all sense of guilt. But whatever the real cause, the fact is before us with frightening clarity: postwar man has no keen sense of sin. And the popularizations of the discoveries of depth psychology and psychiatry go on — with all the errors practically inevitable in any popularization. Hence, more and more of the modern generation are excusing themselves when there is no excuse, and becoming less and less human as they indulge in what they believe to be things perfectly allowable to the emanicipated human.

Some psychologists have led their students to believe that virtue can be explained — and even explained away — in the same manner they have "explained away" sin. "Moral conduct, as it is called," one of them writes, "and immoral conduct, as some still insist on naming it, is nothing but a matter of hormones." Many of them laugh at the idea that man possesses liberty, is endowed with free will, is master of his choices, and, hence, a responsible being. Perhaps without realizing it, they are laughing at the very idea of man, and thus they are sowing very fertile soil with seed that will produce real psychoses and reduce their man to seemingly nothing but a mass of ganglia.

Christ's Church has always taught that heredity, environment, passion, and the existential circumstance, can influence man's choice, and thus, to some extent, limit his liberty. But Christ's Church has never, and will never, deny guilt entirely, nor free one fully from all responsibility, so long as the individual is not completely insane. Christ's Church is "the pillar and ground of truth," and truth is timeless. Catholic truth has always been existential as well as essential. But never the first without the latter. Hence, while granting that man can be more or less responsible in his human acts, it has never made man, so long as he can be called a man, utterly irresponsible. How could it, when it knows man so thoroughly? How could it, when it has God's revelation before it?

When the Prodigal Son came back to his father, he did not say: "My heredity prompted me to ask for my share in the inheritance. My environment made me squander it on harlots." No, it was: "Father, I have *sinned*." When the Son of God had saved the woman caught in adultery from the stoning that was legally due her, He did not say to her: "I know your temperament. I know your drives. I know all your compulsions. So I know you were not to blame for that adultery you were caught in." No, He said: "Go and *sin* no more." Which quite obviously means: "You *did sin* in that act of adultery. You knew you were doing something offensive to God."

That is what sin is: an act that calls for a clear, knowing mind,

and a will that can choose freely. God has told us often enough
that we are endowed with such faculties. We are fully aware of
them ourselves. Yet, lest there be any possibility of self-deception,
God has been most explicit about sin being a reality. God died
because of that reality. And God told some men that they would
die in that very reality. Jesus said to some Jews very bluntly:
"You will die in your sins." When they questioned Him about it,
He repeated His prediction: "If you do not believe that I am he,
you must die in your sins" (Jn 8:24).

So there can be no doubt about it: there is such a thing as sin.
It brought death to the God-Man. It can bring eternal death to
men who are made in the image of God. Since all sin begins in
the mind, but is committed essentially through the will, we are
given what may be a real insight in why it was that the Passion
began with that mystery-filled mental agony which took place in
the Garden of Gethsemani. There we see the Mind and Will of
this Normal Man work in a way that tells us how to be normal,
and how to be men. Today this mystery merits special study; for
it holds the secret of both sanity and sanctity for all of us. It can
even show us the intimate relation between the two!

"Taking Peter, James, and John with him," says St. Mark, "he
gave way to terror and weariness, and said to them: 'I am plunged
in sorrow enough to break my heart. Stay here and keep awake' "
(Mk 14:33, 34).

See all that those lines teach us. First, this Man of all men
"gave way to terror." Consequently, fear in itself, even to the point
of terror, is not abnormal. So long as there is due proportion between cause and effect, so long as there is a real relation between
the object and our reaction, we will be as normal as was the Norm
for all men, Jesus.

Look at the proportion in His case. . . . Why was He "plunged
in sorrow enough to break His Heart"? — because of what was
before Him. He knew what this night would generate, and the
morrow bring forth. He was the all-pure God as well as the
all-perfect Man. Hence it was that with the clear eyes of Infinite
Purity he saw all the filth of mankind's sins rise up like some
mountainous tidal wave and sweep toward Him. It grew as it

came on; it curved over and threatened to break above Him. He knew that once it did break He would be stench itself. He would be sin. Hideous to the eyes of the Father, revolting to the eyes of the Spirit, a repulsive horror to His own clear-sighted gaze. It was not the wide sea of physical sufferings in which He would soon be engulfed that sent Him to His knees begging the Father to spare Him. Because His was a flawless imagination, He all but felt the blow on the cheek that would stagger Him in the home of the high priest that very night; He also felt the sharp bite of the scourges as they curled around His back, and the piercing points of the thorn helmet that would be His on the morrow. But it was not these that had Him crying: "Abba, Father, you can do all things! Spare me this cup!" (Mk 14:36.) Nor was it the shame that would surge through Him as He stood before Pilate, before Herod, before the soldiers in the Praetorium, before the shouting mobs on the way to Calvary, and before the mockers on that Hill of Skulls, that had Him crying out again and again: "Father . . . spare me this cup!" (Lk 22:42.) It was not even the nakedness in which He would stand on Golgotha. It was rather the nakedness of His soul, the nakedness that would be His once He had "been made sin for us." There was perfect proportion then between the sorrow He felt and the object that caused the "almost Heartbreak." It was normal.

Certainly, Christ dreaded the physical torments He knew to be ahead; but it was the deeper torments of the spirit that had Him rising from prayer, staggering back to the three He had invited to share this hour with Him, and almost pleading with them for empathy. Christ was lonely. Christ was afraid. Christ was normal.

The lesson is unmistakable. No human will ever pass through a full life on earth without being, at one time or another, both lonely and afraid. It is normal, as we learn from the Normal Man, Christ. He knew a loneliness, such as no human will ever know again, there in the Garden, despite the presence of the three Apostles. The persistence of His cry: "Abba, Father!" is an anticipation of that soul-shaking cry which will pierce the deepening gloom above the Hill of Skulls. Christ Jesus felt as abandoned in the Garden as He would no Golgotha when from the depths of His being He would cry: "My God, My God, why do you abandon me?" (Mk 15:34).

But it was not until He had looked and seen the futility of it all for so many that He knew a sense of frustration such as no man, nor all men together, could ever know. Christ was Man, but He was also God. He knew! He knew that this night, all of the next day, and the three days that would follow, would be naught but wasted effort on the part of the Son of God for many a son of Adam and many a daughter of Eve. He knew that His Body would be given, and all of His Blood poured out in vain for more than one child of His Father. That is why St. Luke has to report that "Now his struggle became intense, and he prayed the more earnestly, so that his sweat became like clots of blood that fell to the ground" (Lk 22:44).

You and I, and every man, will know anguish, at one time or another, as we watch our best efforts nullified. That is the time for us to look at the Norm for every man, as He experiences such an agony of futility and frustration. The normality in such an event is in the perfect proportion between the cause and the effect. Jesus Christ knew He was about to give the greatest possible proof of His personal love for each individual man — He also knew that for many a man it would all be as fruitless as if He, the Son of God, had never become the Son of Man.

There are days when the front page of a city newspaper with its reports of sin can make the God-conscious man cringe, even as his soul fills with sympathy for the God of Love. To God, however, "a thousand years are as a day." Christ was God. Think, then, what a thousand years of such days would have shown Christ as He sweated in Gethsemani. Every sin, from the first by Eve to the last as time ends, was before Him. Think of the murders, the fratricides (and every murder is such!) that came before Him, from the first by Cain unto the last; think of the lies, the lusts, the greeds, the hates, the pride, the barbarities, and the brutalities of mankind, from those before the Deluge to the end of the world. Christ saw them all — yours and mine among them. He would have to *"become sin"* for us — He would do so — but for some it would be as if He had never existed.

Since love is greatest when it is given freely and fully with no thought of return; since love is at its highest and best when it is naught but sheer, naked, self-giving; then it is love that you hear when you hear Christ end His agony, rid Himself of all paralyzing terror, quiet His breaking Heart, and cease His plea to be spared this cup with His generous *Fiat*.

The contrast must not be missed. So look first at Christ as He staggers back to the drowsing three again and again with fear filling His eyes. Understand His beggar's prayer for human sympathy as He pleads with Peter, James, and John to stay awake while He is lonely, afraid, and filled with a sense of frustration. Then look at this same Christ after His *Fiat*. He comes before the veritable mob that Judas had led out, and with all the calmness of Majesty asks: "Whom seek ye?" When they say: "Jesus of Nazareth," hear Him reply — this Man who was just now sweating blood in fear — "I am he. Therefore, since you are looking for me, let these men go unmolested." This is the same Jesus who a moment ago was seeking sympathy from His sleeping Apostles. A moment later, when Peter strikes off the ear of one of the servants of the high priest, this same Jesus who a few moments before was begging His Father to spare Him the cup, says: "Put the sword back into the sheath. Shall I not drink the cup which the Father has presented to me?" (Jn 18:11.) What a contrast!

Since the mysteries of Christ, which followed on the Son of God coming into flesh, must be lived, some way or other, by everyone who has been redeemed by that Flesh, it is essential that we study all of Christ's mysteries, especially this one of the Agony in the Garden; for no man will ever escape his own hour in this Grotto at Gethsemani.

Some few will be invited, as were Peter, James, and John, to a greater and more intimate share in this mystery. They will have to be more sincere in their *Fiat* than these three favorites seem to have been. Pascal's words, "Jesus Christ will be in Agony until the end of the world" and must ever haunt the real lover of the God-Man . . . "we must not sleep the while!"

We of the present day have been made more aware of the neurotics and psychotics in our civilization than any generation before us. Nevertheless, for every genuine neurotic, and for each psychotic who has lucid moments, as well as for the many border-line cases, Christ has given a perfect example in the Garden, which, if followed, will effect as much good therapy as any known to man — and I daresay even more.

You have just seen the change His *Fiat* wrought in the "per-sonality" of the Son of Man. It can work a somewhat similar change in the personality of every man, and especially of every Christian man. For it gives a different orientation of mind to suffering, even as it gives a totally different direction to his will. And since we have already seen that it takes mind and will to make a man a sinner, it takes mind and will to make a man a saint.

"Have this mind in you which was also in Christ Jesus" (Phil 2:5) is a directive each of us can take as given to us personally. "Mind" in this passage means both faculties of the soul: mind and will. Christ in the Grotto shows us His Mind and Will. It tells us that He was not only accepting the Father's Will, but He was making a total commitment, a donation of His entire being, to that Will of the Father. Thus Christ shows Himself as Obedient Love — and Loving Obedience. That is what you and I and every man living must be if we would become our best self.

The mental sufferings of Christ, undoubtedly, were more cruel than all His physical pains in the Passion. Real thorns pierced His sacred brow, but the thorns that pierced His soul were the ones that brought His Blood to Gethsemani's grass. Since Christ's Passion must be shared in some way by every man, it is not surprising that we have so many mentally ill persons in our society. They, in some sense, are the privileged ones; for, like Peter, James, and John, they have been invited to greater intimacy with Christ. They have been asked into the Grotto to share His mental anguish. Hence, they, perhaps more than others, must learn how to say, how to mean, how to live *Fiat*. If they do, they will be conformed to Christ and greatly gladden the Father who is God.

Obedience by "nothingness," to the first *Fiat* of God brought light into being. Obedience by Mary, expressed in another *Fiat,* brought the Light of the world into Flesh. Obedience to God by that Light, expressed again by a *Fiat,* brought an end to the real darkness that filled the world and burst open those gates through which mortal man may now approach "Light Inaccessible." Obedience by you, by me, by any man, can bring sanity, sanctity, and perfect conformity to the Mind and Will of Christ.

There is only one passport that is recognized by Him who stands at the portals of Heaven. It is the *stigmata of Christ.* We must have them if we would gain Bliss. If they are not on our bodies, then they must be in our minds. That is what mental sufferers are to realize: they bear in their minds the marks of Christ! Hence they should rejoice in being granted such intimacy and say *Fiat* with readier will and more loving heart.

To those who are not so privileged comes the question: How do you see the genuine neurotics and the true psychotics of our day? Is it as special favorites of God who are asked to bear the stigmata of Christ in their souls rather than on their bodies? Do we stand before them as Francis of Assisi once stood before a leper — and, looking through appearances, recognize in them the Lord Jesus Christ? He is in these people, suffering as He suffered in the Grotto at Gethsemani. Perhaps, because of our blindness, He has to cry in them today as He never cried in Gethsemani. Perhaps He is saying again in them: *"Eloi, Eloi, lama sabachthani!"* Christ can be very lonely in these suffering humans . . . "we must not sleep the while!"

Mental affliction can overwhelm us — and will, if we do not pray this prayer which came from Christ when He was all but overwhelmed by mental affliction. *Fiat* lived — that is, not sounding merely from our lips, but shaping our whole lives — would greatly help us to preserve the sanity with which to become saintly. Better, it would enable us to "fill up what is wanting to the Passion of Christ" and thus enable us to become what we are supposed to be — the *pleroma Christi.*

*Fiat* makes one strong with the strength of Christ. We need that strength, for if we do not merit the intimacy to be allowed a share in His mental agony, we most assuredly will be granted a share in the mystery of His physical Passion. We must walk the way to Glory — He is *the Way.*

# CHAPTER TEN

# The Mystery of the Way and Our Oneness

~~~~~~~~~~~~~~~~~~~~~~~~~~~~~~~~~~~~~

## *Ecce Homo!* — Look! He *Is* a Man!

As WE contemplate Christ as He stands before Pilate, and hear this Roman governor saying: *"Ecce Homo!"* — "Look! He *is* a Man!" we feel more than pity. We are awed and baffled. For the bloodied, brutally beaten Figure before us, though obviously scourged to within a stroke of death, though crowned with mocking thorns, and with human spittle — that ignominy of ignominies — on His face, stands with a majesty immeasurable, a dignity indefinable, and seems both above it all and outside it all. Though we cannot grasp all there is in and about the Prisoner, we can grasp very easily why Pilate said: *"Ecce Homo!"* He himself could hardly believe his eyes. He had to exclaim: "Look! This spectacle in blood and rags and spittle *is* a man!"

It is quite obvious that, at this juncture in the proceedings, Pilate was endeavoring to stir up pity for the Man who had been brought to him that morning as One worthy of death. It can hardly be doubted that the sight of Jesus, after the scourging, mocking, and crowning, shocked Pilate. He wanted to save this Man from the Cross. He knew the Jews had delivered Him up out of envy, and, as a Roman governor, he had little patience with such petty tactics. As he looked at Jesus in that scarlet cloak, under that crown of thorns, with the mocking reed in His hands, Pilate himself must have been moved to pity. Luke tells us that "Pilate spoke to them again, wishing to release Jesus" (Lk 23:20).

Unquestionably Christ was an object for pity at that moment. He did not look much like a man, far less like a king. As for

Him being one to "pervert the nation," never did any human look more powerless than this whipped Prisoner whose hands were tied and whose tongue would not be loosed. But were appearances ever more deceptive? At the very moment of the *Ecce Homo!* God the Father was looking on His Son with greater love, if such a thing were possible in God, than when He looked on Him on Thabor, and, undoubtedly, could have said the same thing: "Behold, this is My Son, in whom I am very well pleased!" He might even have said something like: "Behold, I make all things new!" (Ap 21:5.) For this *was* the beginning of making everything new; this was the Re-creation. It began with Mary's *"Ecce ancilla. .. ."* It went on with John the Baptist's *"Ecce Agnus Dei."* It neared its climax as Christ Himself said: *"Ecce ascendimus . . .* Behold, we go up to Jerusalem, where the Son of Man will be betrayed . . ." (Mt 20:18). He had foretold it all, but even His most intimate friends did not understand what was foretold. Now it was fact. Christ hardly looked human. But was He ever more divine? This was love in action. This was loving "unto the end."

Pilate had used every dodge possible: he had sent Christ to Herod, only to have Him sent back robed as a fool! He had offered the noisy rabble a choice between Christ and one he felt sure they would never choose: Barabbas. Finally, in what looks like desperation, he had Christ scourged. The soldiers had added their own touches with the cloak, the scepter, and the crown of thorns. *"Ecce Homo!"* said Pilate; but, with ever mounting fury, the cry came: "Crucify him! Crucify him!" When Pilate sensed that he could never silence them, he "released Barabbas to please them, but turned Jesus over . . . to crucifixion."

To us, in this twentieth century, the injustice of it all is palpable. The more we meditate it, the greater our horror and indignation. We think such an outrage could never be perpetrated again. But how wrong we are! "Jesus Christ will be in agony until the end of the world."

Since you know that the Mystical Body of Christ is the reality of realities in this day of ours, you must have heard the voices of modern Pilates saying hundreds of times exactly what Rome's representative said in that long ago. Christ is our contemporary.

He has stood before numerous crowds as shackled, as mocked and spit upon, almost as cruelly scourged, a thousand times and more in this century. But not many modern judges try to do what Pilate tried to do on the first Good Friday of history. Not many are striving to stir up pity for Jesus. Not many are endeavoring to release Him. Not many are saying *"Ecce Homo!"* the way Pilate said it, or for the same purpose. But *you* can look and you can see Christ in His members who are being persecuted as was the historical Christ almost 2000 years ago.

We need to look at the contemporary Christ and recognize Him for who He is. We shudder at the Gospel narratives of the trials of the historical Christ. We shudder as we read of what the Roman emperors did in that "Age of Persecution" to the infant Mystical Body. But what have we witnessed since atheistic Communism came onto history's stage? Nero, Diocletian, Trajan, and Vespacian were gentle compared to those who work the same deeds in our twentieth century. It began early in Russia, as soon as Marxism had gained some hold. It has not ceased from that day to this. Nor is it likely to so long as atheism is its doctrine and militancy its mode.

As Communism has spread, so has the persecution of Christ. Has He been allowed so much as a cattle cave and a cattle manger in any of the countries that have gone Communistic? Russia was only the beginning — bitter as it was. China followed suit. Now, after Europe and Asia, we are seeing the same pattern being followed in Africa, in South America, Central America, and even off the coast of North America. We are living in a New Age of Persecution. In Africa, and other parts of the world, you will hear talk against "colonialism" and the "foreigner." These are but tags under which they are actually persecuting Christ. History, in this particular instance, does repeat itself. It was under these same tags that the historical Christ was done to His Death. For it was as a political menace that the scribes and high priests first presented Christ to Pilate. Ultimately, it was but a political move on Pilate's part — after the Scourging and Crowning — that sent Christ to His Cross.

But just as beyond all "tags" then there was the working out of the master plan of the Father, the love of the Son, and the workings of the Holy Spirit, so today, beyond all the tags, political, sociological, and ideological, the same Christ — but now in and through His mystical members — is doing the same wondrous work He was about that day He stood on Pilate's balcony.

Praise be to God for the fact that in many of His members the same majestic calm is found. For, like Christ that morning of the Crucifixion, these Mystical members know exactly what is going on beneath the appearances. Like Christ they have prayed, "Abba, Father, all things are possible to thee. Let this chalice pass!" But again like Christ they have given an all-potent *Fiat*.

These are your brothers who have suffered. These are your fellow members in that Body of which Christ is the Head who have stood as bloody, buffeted, and beaten as stood the Christ Himself. So this is your mystery as well as theirs! This is the "Passion of Christ" today. There is only one Christ — the Whole Christ, as St. Augustine was so fond of calling Him. Consequently, on any day of your life, since before the second decade in this present century, the Voice that rang out over Saul, as he lay prostrate outside the city of Damascus, could have rung out over many a modern city and asked the same question: "Why do you persecute me?" If any of the modern persecutors would ask what Saul asked that day, "Who art thou, Lord?" the identical reply would have come from the Heavens: "I am Jesus whom you are persecuting" (Acts 9:4–6). For, as philosophy teachers, it is the person who suffers or acts.

Two parallel happenings reveal to you how near God is. Look at St. John's account of what happened in the house of the high priest, Annas, and what happened to Saul outside Damascus. When the chief priest questioned Jesus about His teachings, He replied: "I have spoken openly, where all the world could listen. . . . I have said nothing in secret. Why do you question me? Question those who heard what I said." This was the only proper reply to make; for the entire proceeding was illegal, and Christ, in His kindness, was trying to let them know how illegal it all was. But He had no sooner performed this truly good deed than a guard who stood by "gave him a blow on the face and said: 'Is this the way you answer the chief priest?' Jesus protested. 'If I was wrong in speaking this way, then prove me wrong; but if I was right, then why do you strike me?' " (Jn 18:19–23.)

In the hall of Annas the blow fell on His physical Body. He, the Person who owned that Body, cried out: "Why do you strike me?" When Saul was persecuting the members of Christ's Mystical Body, the blows fell on the Body, but the Person who owns that Body is the same who cried out: "Saul, Saul, why persecutest thou me?" The same Person, then, was struck — once in His physical members, second in His mystical members; and the same Person made the same complaint: "Why strike me?" Obviously, we are one with Christ! Hence, over almost any road, in any city under the sun, the same Voice Saul heard on the road to Damascus could have rung out, and with the same question.

The contemporary Christ has stood before modern Pilates all over the world, and often He has stood as bedraggled in His members of His Mystical Body as He stood bedraggled in His physical Body. There is a difference however. Pilate hoped to stir up some pity. Not so modern Pilates! When they turn to the mob — for that is precisely what makes up the so-called Peoples' Court — and say *"Ecce homo!"* it is not to stir up any pity for the prisoner, but to bring forth the chant the mob has been taught to give: "Away with him! Away with him! Crucify him!" They use different words, but they mean the same thing. The modern epithets of "capitalist" — "foreign devil" — "obstructionist" — "deviationist" — and the like, have as much validity as did the charges laid before Pilate: "perverter of the nation" — "rebellionist" — "enemy to Caesar."

Into my Trappist cloister have come some of the priests who have had the glory of suffering under the Communists. To look into eyes that had known such pain, and hear the living voices describing their part in that Passion of Christ, which will go on until the end of time, was to feel the closest fellowship with them "in Christ Jesus," and with Christ Jesus in them.

Christ has been scourged, spat upon, mocked, and crowned in almost countless bishops, priests, brothers, nuns, and laity behind those curtains of iron and bamboo. He could have been seen in those who were marched to death in North Korea, in those still imprisoned throughout the sprawling country called the Peoples' Republic of China. To see nuns in prison garb is to see Christ in His more delicate members wearing today the fool's robe He wore the day He came back to Pilate's Praetorium after having been in Herod's Court.

How do you react to all this persecution? These are your brothers. You will not shrug your shoulders as did Cain and ask: "Am I my brother's keeper?" These are your fellow members in the one Body of Christ. They are *your* members mystically. Hence com-passion in their real passion is the only proper reaction.

I felt this some fifteen years ago when word came that my own Trappist brothers, high in the mountains of North China, had been dragged before the Annases and Caiphases of Chinese Communism, and subjected to every indignity the Oriental mind could devise.

Our Lady of Consolation was an abbey founded in North China by French Trappists in 1883. The summer of 1947 saw that abbey closed. Red soldiers lined up the seventy-five monks (only five of whom were not Chinese!) and, as morning broke, marched them off to a Peoples' Court.

Before more than a thousand Chinese peasants, who had been coralled from all the villages in the district, these seventy-five monks were tried. When charges as groundless as those hurled against Christ when He stood before Pilate brought the truth-filled reply of "Not guilty!" instead of hearing anything such as Christ heard about "What is truth?" they heard their "judge" command that they be clubbed.

Christ's scourging at the pillar was brutality itself. So was this clubbing of these Trappist priests who had done as much wrong as Christ had done as He "went about doing good." These monks had not "gone about" — their rule of cloister prevented that. But they had done so much good while remaining within their cloister that the Chinese of the district had had two bronze tablets struck, one of which read: "The benefits you have brought us are as weighty as the mountains." The other held this verdict: "No matter how closely scrutinized, your kindness has always been found to be uniform." The people of the district whenever speaking of the abbey always referred to it as "an instrument of goodness and mercy."

When the judges asked the people for their verdict, these same peasants, who had had those tablets of bronze struck, cried out as did the Jews at Jerusalem that first Good Friday of time. They did not say: "Crucify them!" but they did equivalently say: "Away with them" as they rendered their verdict that these monks were "enemies of the people" whose sentence had to be: "They deserve to die — all of them."

"In Christ Jesus" these men are your brothers, they are your fellow members of the One Body, as close to you mystically as your hand is to your arm anatomically. St. Paul was unceasing in his insistence on our oneness "in Christ Jesus"; and told us again and again that if one member rejoiced, all should rejoice, if one member suffered, all should feel some pain. Oneness in Christ is a reality.

If you are alive to the oneness of Christ in His Mystical Body, you will anguish over your brothers and sisters who are suffering so in the hostile part of the world in the service of Christ. You, and I, and every other member of His Mystical Body, should be as deeply moved by the news of their suffering as every American was moved by the news of President Kennedy's assassination. It is well to remind ourselves that the missionaries are far closer to us as members of the Mystical Body than John F. Kennedy was as a member of that body politic of America, even though he was our President. The bond between us and those missionaries is "quasi physical," it is truly mystical. The bond between us citizens of the United States is at best only moral. We all were stunned that sad Friday in November, 1963. We should be more deeply stunned when we hear of anything like the persecution of the Christian missionaries. For if we love Christ, we will love them "in Christ." If we love them truly, the atrocities they have undergone will come home to us as personal afflictions.

Among the deepest mysteries in your life and in mine is our oneness with all other humans. We are related to all others physically through origin from the same First Parents. We are related to all mystically by reason of the Will of God to unite all under the one Head — Christ. That is why the mad happenings in this mad century can never leave us unmoved. "If one member is in pain, all members share it. If one member is honored, all the members share its satisfaction" (1 Cor 12:26). The closeness of the members and the oneness of the whole should be in your consciousness steadily. You have had experiences of this oneness in the body politic of late, and should easily make the comparison between what is merely a moral oneness to the oneness that is more than moral, a oneness that is "quasi physical." When John Glenn made his successful orbital flight, did you not walk a little taller, feel bigger and better? Of course. We all did. For we all shared in the glory, the thrill of it all, because we are Americans. We are one. And when our President was murdered, did not a piece of you die? Of course. Every true American, no matter what his political affiliations, no matter what his personal relations and reaction to the Kennedys, shared in the tragedy of that day as truly as they breathed the same air of earth. As Catholics, then, do you not die a bit daily when you see Christ mystically scourged, crowned, mocked, spit upon, and exhibited to howling mobs with the challenge in Pilate's words: *"Ecce homo!"* You are knit more closely to Christ and His members than you can ever be to your country or your fellow citizens. Compassion is born of contemplation of this reality; for a consciousness of your closeness to Christ blows to brilliant flame the tiniest spark of love for God that rests in any soul! If you do not and cannot feel compassion for His members, then, at least, you will feel it for Him, the Head.

We Trappists had monasteries in Germany, Yugoslavia, Hungary, Poland, Holland, Belgium, and France in 1935. But from 1935 to 1945 our civilization went through the Nazi nightmare. Practically every country in Europe suffered physically from the delusions of grandeur entertained by the egomaniac house painter from Austria. Silent monks learned by sad experience what it was to be arrested, face hostile judges, hear utterly groundless charges, stand before juries already foresworn, and listen to condemnations so palpably unjust as to baffle the stunned mind of the lowest among the animals called rational. Thus it was that these monks learned what it means to live in the Mystical Body of Christ; what it means to share in the mysteries of His Passion. They knew scourges and thorns. They learned by experience the unbelievable horrors excogitated for them by the subhumans who ran Hitler's concentration camps.

Did you ever once think, while the Jews were undergoing those unbelievable tortures and those hideous deaths, did you once think while these atrocities were being perpetrated, that your Lord and God was a Jew; that your Immaculate Mother was the Lily of Israel, the very Glory of her people who were Jews? Did you once recall that the Apostles and all the earliest martyrs were Jews? Did you realize then that Pius XI was definite about your relation to all those who were being burned in these chambers? He said that all of us Catholics are "spiritually Semites." "In Christ Jesus" you and I were being tried in Germany, exiled in Holland, cast into prison at Dachau, and cast into furnaces at Auschwitz and Buchenwald. "If one member is in pain, all the members share it" (1 Cor 12:26). All the cruelty in this cruel century is part of the mystery that makes you and me what we are, and part of the mysteries that make our life. It is Christ in us who is reliving His mysteries, and we in Him, our Contemporary, who are "filling up what is wanting."

Now it may be that you and I will never be tied to any pillar physically, or feel the lash bite into our flesh; nevertheless, you and I are going to live these mysteries of Christ in all reality. We must. For there is only one way to the Father, one way to Glory, one way to Bliss — the way He walked.

If we are spared the Scourging and Crowning physically, we will not be spared them mystically; for God has but one pattern for all His children. He used it for His only Son. He will use it for His every son; for Christ was "the firstborn of many brethren," and all His brethren must live like the firstborn.

Without doubt you have already had some share in these two mysteries. Through injustice in your life you have had a share in the second and third Sorrowful Mysteries in the life of Christ. If you have not met injustice, let me assure you that you will; for the Sorrowful Mysteries in the life of Christ must make up the mysteries in the life of every Christian. That, too, is revelation. Read the fifteenth chapter of St. John's Gospel and you will be reading your future; you will be reading it as foretold by Christ Himself at His Last Supper. "If you were children of the world," He said, "the world would cherish its own flesh and blood. But you are not children of the world; on the contrary, I have singled you out from the world, and therefore the world hates you. Remember what I told you: a slave is not better than his master. If they persecuted me, they will persecute you also . . . it is because you profess my name that they will treat you in all these ways" (Jn 15:18–21).

That is not a very pleasant prospect — until we realize that when the world hates us, and wreaks its hatred by persecuting us, then we are truly His members who walked this way we are now on, and walked it to Glory!

Christ said: "Learn of me; for I am meek and humble of heart" (Mt 11:29). The humility of God is what offset, and will yet offset, the pride of man. That is the humility you and I must cultivate; for, as we have already seen, Christ's life is aptly summed up as "humility expressed in obedience — and such obedience is a perfect act of love." But we become humble only one way: by suffering humiliations. That is one of the hardest of all lessons for any child of Adam to learn. In point of fact, we cannot learn it as children of Adam. We have to become sons of God and learn it from, in, and through God's only Son. Once we have learned from Him, then we will welcome humiliations just because we are His members whose life was one long humiliation.

As you hear in your heart the Roman governor's words, "Look, he is a Man," do as he commands: look at the Man — *Ecce Homo!* and realize you are looking at your God humbled to the last and lowest degree. There He stands in His kenotic plenitude: fully empty! Then, above the din of the mob, hear Christ's own command to you: "Master my lessons . . . Thus you will find refreshment for your soul" (Mt 11:29, 30).

When your face is made to burn because of some humiliation, master His lesson. When your blood surges to your head because of some stinging taunt, master His lesson. When you are insulted by some nasty name, and your whole being rises up in indignation, master His lesson. He, the Son of God, was called a devil! He, the Wisdom of God, was treated as a fool! He, the Splendor of the Father's glory, was slapped in the face and had His sacred countenance befouled by spittle from a savage soldiery. He, the Only Omnipotent, had His hands tied by mere men. He, the all-pure Spirit, was stripped naked and scourged. He, the King of kings, was mocked as regal and crowned with thorns. Of that Scourged Body, and that Crowned Head, you are a member.

You will share in this Second and in this Third Sorrowful Mystery — maybe even physically; for Communism is in our hemisphere, on our continent, in our own land. It may yet do here what it has already done over half the inhabited globe: it may scourge Christ actually, put the robe of a fool on Him, laugh at, spit upon, and make mockery of the Son of God as it crowns Him with thorns — in His mystical members.

You may be one of those members thus honored by God — and outraged by men. If so, what a glory will be yours! But even if you do not share in these mysteries physically, be assured that you will know your full share in them spiritually; for this is the Way — the only Way — to the Father — and to Glory. You are in that Way.

# CHAPTER ELEVEN

# The Mystery of the Only Choice

*"He Who Is Not With Me . . ."*

HAS God abandoned us to ourselves?

That query is inescapable for any man or woman who looks and sees what has been going on, and what is now being done in our world.

We know that God cannot die. We know He does not sleep. But we also know that He can leave mankind to mankind's own resources. Has He done so to us of the twentieth century?

Studying those events in our century that will be recorded in history, and noting the marks left by them on the men of this century, we have reason to ask if God has abandoned us. Has He left us to our own slim resources? We know His respect for the liberty with which He endowed us. But we wonder if He is so weary of the ways we have used it that He is just letting us go our way.

We have touched the topic of the only choice some men have found in life. It is the same as Hamlet's: "To be or not to be." But the men of our century have not been as rational, nor as religious, as was Hamlet; they do not consider, as did he, the fact that God has "fixed His canon against self-slaughter." There are many suicides. For after the madness we call World War I, there followed a deeper madness evidenced by the immorality in both public and private life. Immorality is found in the wake of every war. But so much of it arose in France and Germany in the second decade of this century, that some of the best minds in each country came to the conclusion that the only choice left a thinking man was suicide or mockery. There was much mockery. There were many,

many suicides. All that would never have been if men had learned to listen to the Good News — the Gospel of Christ — and been made aware of the only choice man is really allowed so long as he is on earth. It is not between suicide and mockery, but between . . . well, there are countless ways of phrasing this one choice. You may call it a choice between loving rightly, which means loving God, and loving wrongly, which means a false self-love; or you can say it is a choice between measuring up to the Normal Man, Christ, or being abnormal, using as your yardstick the temporal, the human, the material. You can say it is a choice between self-control, self-denial, selflessness or self-centeredness, self-satisfaction, naked, unashamed, selfishness. You might even say it is a choice between being saint or sinner, wise or foolish, a builder for time or for eternity. There are, as I said, countless ways of phrasing the choice, but the best, the clearest, the definitely challenging way was put by God Himself: "He who is not with me is against me, and he who does not gather with me scatters" (Mt 12:30). That is the one choice every man is to make: to be with Christ or against Him. That is the ultimate. No man can be neutral. If we are not gathering with Christ, we are most certainly scattering. If we are not "filling up what is wanting" we are wasting time, scattering talents, emptying life of all content and human existence of all true humanness and all real meaning. We are given the one choice between collaborating with God in His providence, co-redeeming with Christ in His Passion, cooperating with God the Holy Spirit as He "renews the face of the earth" — or turning our back on the Three-Personed God and going our own way.

As we look about us today, we begin to surmise that the men of our century have made their choice — and it has not been to be with Christ. But even as the surmise takes shape we are conscious of two conflicting thoughts: Has God abandoned us? and Has Christ failed in His promise? He did say: "I am with you at all times as long as the world will last" (Mt 28:20).

Ours is a changing world, but our God is changeless, and He is the Lord of the universe. Men may be faithless, but the fidelity of our God can never be questioned. So Christ must be with us. But are we with Him?

We know that after World War I the philosophy of Nihilism took the forefront. After World War II, the same thing under a different name took over. *Nausea* was but a mild reaction to the realities thinkers looked upon. Despair was the deeper reaction; and it was not confined to the few. It was, and it is, an inevitable reaction for anyone who looks and sees only the surface of things. To stay sane in this changing world of ours one has to look deep down into things and see, looking up from all this suffering, the face of Christ. He is with us — He always will be. But we have to make the deliberate choice to be with Him.

What is the reality of all realities in life? The choice allowed man either to "crucify Christ again" (Heb 6:6) or "crucify our own flesh with its passionate cravings" (Gal 5:25). If that be not *the* reality of earth, then truly Christ has been unfaithful to His promise. For you have seen what men have done to men and are still doing. They tried to reduce Cardinal Mindszenty to the level of a dog. They endeavored to take the very soul out of him; and leave him with only animal reactions to the stimuli to which they tried to condition him — just as Pavlov had done with his dogs in his early experiments. They have "brainwashed" many a human, reducing them to the level of a robot, a mere mechanical man who does not think but simply echoes like a parrot or mimics like a monkey. They have indoctrinated youth in such a fashion that many a young adult and most of the adolescents in their countries know nothing of their origin nor anything of original sin. Consequently, they have heard naught about Redemption which is already wrought and Salvation which they should be working out. These hapless youngsters know nothing of the Father or their true eternal Fatherland. You have seen men destroy man by first destroying, as far as that is possible, Him who made man. You have seen brazen godlessness. You have seen it in all its insulting aggressiveness. You have seen men who defied manhood and mankind, by pronouncing themselves militant atheists. That means that you have seen men go mad. But it is one thing to realize that God has abandoned some men to their madness; it is another, a better, a clearer-visioned thing to look below the surface of all the madness in our century and see there the providence of God, the face of Christ, the fidelity of our Lover. He has kept His promise. He is with us. The frenzy of our day is but the fulfillment of His prediction made at His Last Supper. The world is full of hate because it is full of Christ and Christians. That is the reality. Hence, we touch reality when beneath the features of the broken Cardinal Mindszenty we see the Man of Sorrows as He stumbles to the Hill of Skulls. We see what is really going on when in the agonized face of the martyrs we recognize the countenance of the agonizing Christ. "Christ shall be in agony until the end of time . . ." and you are His member!

If we fail to recognize the fact that man has only one choice in life, and that is between befriending the Man Pilate condemned to death and being an "enemy to the Cross of Christ," we will be forced to conclude with Pascal that "man is a monster, a chimera, a chaos, the shame of the universe," and agree with Alexander Pope as he says "man is but a jest and a riddle in the world."

But, having read the Message of Joy, which we call the Gospel of Jesus Christ, we should know exactly what is going on in our day. What happened in Jerusalem almost two thousand years ago is being paralleled all over our globe.

Christ is with us. He will be "as long as the world will last." The burning question is: How many men will be with Christ? For that is the only choice allowed us mortals. If we are not with Him, we are against Him — and that means tragedy and eternal death for the ones who make the wrong choice.

That is only just. For Christ died for all men. Every man, then, belongs to Jesus Christ. He paid full price for each. All men are His, then, by right of purchase. He will use them all. We will be wise then if we look on all men as God the Father does, and see in each Him whom the Father looked upon before time was, and upon whom He will look when time ceases to be — the only Son.

It is Christ who suffers in all men who suffer, and Christ who dies in all men who die. It was Christ who suffered in Cardinal Mindszenty. It was Christ who died in President Kennedy that black Friday of late November, 1963. It is Christ who is gripped in every human agony — that of the young couple who see that there first child is stillborn, or, what may be momentarily more agonizing, to see that their child is a mongoloid. It is Christ in them. It is Christ that you can see in every lonely child, in every lost child, in every child who weeps; for it has been wisely said that "there is only one child in all the world — the Christ Child." And it can be as wisely said that in all the universe there is only one human — the Divine-Human, Christ Jesus. He is "with us all days" . . . and He is ever "about His Father's business" which is your salvation.

"If anyone wants to be my follower, he must renounce himself and shoulder his cross day by day; then he may be a follower of mine" (Lk 9:23). That is the challenge of life; that is the choice allowed us in living. As you see, we really have no choice even though we are perfectly free; for he who will not be a follower of Christ must be mad.

You are sane. What is the shape of your cross? Is it merely the numbing humdrum of daily routine? Is it sickness? Is it sorrow for loved ones who are far away, who are not well, who have failed in business, failed in marriage, failed in life? Is it your own failure? your own huge frustration? It really does not matter what its source, we know the shape is always ultimately the same — it is cruciform. But the Cross means Christ! And Christ means joy! Yes, but only if we are alert, alive, filled with love.

"He, in view of the joy offered him, underwent crucifixion. . . ." Thus speaks the Holy Spirit through St. Paul. Joy — that is the Good News. Joy is the substance of Christianity, because joy is the fruit of love, and love is the essence of the legacy left us by Christ. Love is the quintessence of the life He shares with us. That is the "fire" He came to "cast upon the earth." That is the fire that burns in the hearts of all His true members. Love is bigger than life. Love is bigger than death. Love is as big as God — and you are His image. So your life must be love. It will be if you allow the Christ to live and love in you, to suffer and die in you, to rise again in you to Glory.

No matter where you walk in life, you will walk the way of the Fourth Sorrowful Mystery. No matter what your station in society, you will have to make those Stations that are on the Way of the Cross. No one escapes it. For such is the Will of the Father — for all His sons. But there are two ways of walking: one as an "enemy to the Cross of Christ" or as His cheerful, helpful member.

Everyone in the Way of the Cross that first Good Friday helped Christ in one way or another to accomplish Redemption. The soldiers, who lifted the Cross from the Man who had fallen beneath it so that He might struggle on, helped the God-Man toward the completion of His Sacrifice in their way as well as did Simon of Cyrene who actually carried the Cross with Christ. Those who jeered and would cover Him with shame contributed their part to His work of reparation as well as did the weeping women who would cover Him with sympathy. Those who befouled His face with spittle were playing their part in His work of wiping out all sin, as much as Veronica played her part as she wiped that spittle from His face. Man's solidarity in sin is no great mystery when compared with man's solidarity in the mystery that conquered sin.

It is a frightening solidarity. For Caiphas with his cunning counsel that it was to their "advantage that one man should die, so that the whole nation should be saved from ruin" (Jn 11:50); Judas with his avaricious question: "What are you willing to give?" (Mt 26:15) as well as with his traitorous kiss; Herod with his anger at being met with majestic silence and his having the robe of a fool wrapped about Incarnate Wisdom — each contributed to the work of man's Redemption. Pilate with his timidity before the taunts of the leaders, and his cowardice before the cries of the mob, did likewise; as did the very soldiers who carried out the crucifixion. These had their parts to play in the drama of Redemption even as Mary and Joseph and others had their parts to play; for God had ordained that while some would give life and protect it in His only Son, others would take it. What happened then, happens now. Mankind is divided into those who take Christ's life, and those who help Him live so that He may save them.

That truth takes us one step farther into reality and opens our eyes to the fact that all men will attain the end for which they were created — but that attainment will be as different with different men as Heaven is from Hell. In other words, God will get His glory — which is the end for which every man was made — from every man He has made. But, as with the angels, that glory will be taken from some and given by others. God, who "will never give His glory to another" gets His glory from Satan and his followers this very day, just as really as He gets His glory from Christ, Mary, Joseph, and all the other saints of Heaven. So the ultimate choice allowed us humans is not whether we will give God glory or not, but whether we will give it to Him gloriously and gladly from Heaven, or have it taken from us as we hate in Hell. The thrill to living lies in the fact that we are making that choice every day of our lives, and every hour of the day — as we carry our cross willingly, or curse our fate!

When Christ walked His way of the Cross He really did not carry His Cross; He carried ours! Hence, it can be said that you were there that Good Friday. So was I. So was each human who has every lived or who will ever live. For "God made sin of him who knew no sin" (2 Cor 5:21) and "He bore our sins in his own Body on the Cross . . ." (1 Pt 2:24.) The inspired text reads "our sins" — and it is to be taken literally. Adam's sin and Eve's. The sin of Cain — and that of Abel. The sins I committed, and those that are yours. He bore them. He bore them in His Body on the Cross. He made them His own, since God had "made Him sin for us." By a miracle of love the solidarity that is ours in sin became a certain solidarity in Redemption; for we were on the Cross with Christ because of His love taking our sins upon Him. That solidarity leads now to a very definite solidarity in Salvation; for Christ is in us, helping us carry our crosses for the salvation of mankind. We were there then. He is here now. To work Redemption then He used the body and blood Mary gave Him. To work Salvation now He uses our body and blood.

"If you will be my follower . . ." There is no escaping this mystery. It takes various forms and multiple shapes, but it is the one same mystery in every human life. No man is worthy to help God. Yet every man is destined, and has even been predestined, to help the God-Man. For the Passion still goes on. It really is the substance of every man's living. But it is *with Christ* that we are now carrying the Cross, and it is Christ who now carries our crosses with us. For, with Paul, you and I can, and must, say of ourselves: "It is now no longer I who live, but Christ lives in me.

The life I now live in this body, I live by faith in the Son of God, who loved me and sacrificed himself for me" (Gal 2:20).

Christ took the Cross with love. That is the way we should take ours. That does not mean it will not bear us down and even make us bloody. But He struggled on; for always there was joy before Him. So there must be before us.

Meditate on Him who knew no sin, but whom God made sin for us, and you will take up your cross day after day with gratitude and love — even with a sense of justice!

Specifically, just what is your cross? It is the duties of your state in life.

The married have their cross. To love, honor, and obey, as they promised when the Sacrament was administered, and do it for a lifetime, is no easy thing. To be faithful to one until death is no light engagement. But, just as Christ did not come down from His Cross, so Christians, today, can remain on theirs; for their human weakness is bolstered by the strength of Christ, which is Omnipotence, since they can say with Paul: "With Christ I am nailed to the cross." Fully realizing that they can carry their cross not only faithfully, but joyfully.

What joy there is in accomplishment! See what the ordinary man and the ordinary woman accomplish day in and day out so long as they are one with Christ. The housewife washing dishes, sweeping floors, making beds, preparing meals, is helping God save men! The salesman going from prospect to prospect is engaged in a work of cosmic proportions and of eternal import, no matter how unimportant the product he sells, for he is actually prolonging the Incarnation of the only Son, filling up what is wanting to that Son's Passion, and helping God change mankind from a "caravan on the way to death" to a column of happy warriors hurrying on to victory. The most insignificant piece of work, done by the least of all humans, when done "in Christ Jesus" helps heal the wounds of the world, sweetens the sorrows of mankind, glorifies the God of glory.

It may well be that many a mother will have to walk the Way of the Cross as Mary did. They may have to watch *their own* fall in weakness, be stripped naked and shamed in public. They may have to watch their very own die as a criminal. But what will lift that sorrowing mother's heart and steady her on her feet will be the theological reality as recognized by Mary — and as viewed by us in Mary. Mothers who have to watch their innocent children suffer need to learn from Mary how to walk the Way of the Cross. Mothers who have to watch their not-so-innocent ones die as criminals need to learn from Mary how to stand beneath the Cross. All mothers need to learn from Mary how to co-offer and coredeem!

Fathers who may have to walk to a Calvary on which they will watch their son die must realize the death of the Son of God was Redemption! So today for those who are "in Christ Jesus" — what looks like a waste can be Salvation.

Since mankind is no longer a "caravan on the way to death," but the Christ on His way to Resurrection, we can see the Savior of the world walking toward Calvary in every human we encounter. He will not look like "the most beautiful of the sons of men." But He will be the Son of God nonetheless. Consequently, you can be Veronica. I can be a Cyrenean. We all can be like Mary: we can collaborate, cooperate, co-offer, and coredeem. But it will take faith.

It will take faith to clear our eyes so that we can recognize Christ as He passes by. It will take charity to love those who appear unlovable. But we have that faith, and we have that charity, for we are His members, and His members are animated by the Spirit of Love.

That is the mystery in your life: you can see in every suffering human the ever suffering Christ; you can minister to the Son of God in every son of man; you can come face to face with the Divine in every feature that is human. The mystery deepens when you realize that you, who are ever in need of being saved, can actually help God save others by your every action and all your suffering. You can enjoy vision where others may not even have sight; for in the most ugly of humans you will see and recognize that "beauty ever ancient, ever new" — the beauty of God.

It is not the good alone who carry the cross. Every man does. Consequently, it is not only the winsomeness of youth that calls out to us to help them with their burden in life, but also the old — and not infrequently the crabbed and ever complaining old — who cannot seem to let life's burden down, nor carry it with any grace. They are falling beneath their cross. They need our assistance. Rather it is Christ who needs us; for it is He in them who stumbles on His Way to Calvary.

Christ is suffering in the rich as well as in the poor, in the well fed as well as in the starving. He walks toward Calvary in those who dwell in mansions just as really as He does in those who live in slums. Christ is walking all the ways of the world, and each of them is a Way of the Cross. We can help Him or not. That is the choice we have in life.

But what of your own cross? It is joy; for just as you were there when Christ carried His Cross, so is He here when you are carrying yours. Realize that as you stumble toward Golgatha you are actually stumbling toward Glory! I dare say you will fall on the way. But just as Redemption was wrought by Him who fell and got up, so salvation will be won by those who fall but get up and go on. No man will ever go to Hell for having fallen. He alone goes there who falls and *stays down*. You and I never need stay down; for Omnipotence is at our side, supporting our elbow, lifting us up — for He needs our weakness so that He may yet save the world of men whom He has already redeemed. That it is which makes the most sorrowful mystery in our lives a mystery that is filled with joy.

# CHAPTER TWELVE

## The Mystery of the End Which Is a Beginning

~~~~~~~~~~~~~~~~~~~~~~~~~~~~~~~~~~~~~~~~~~~~~~~~~~~~~~~~~~~~

*". . . How Wonderful, I Live Forever and Ever."*

By NOW you must be ready to admit that "in mystery you live, and move, and have your being." But, though we have seen many of the mysteries in your life, we have not seen all, nor are we going to: they are too numerous for any book. Your very being, your birth, your prenatal existence have been mysteries, but you did find some solution when you found yourself a thought in the Eternal Mind, a definite, determined object of love by the Ever-lasting Will. Life itself is a tremendous mystery, but you learned at least the purpose of it from Him who gave it to you as He spoke through the writings of St. Paul. Love has been the key to all your mysteries. But now you come to face a mystery toward which you, like every human before and about you, have been heading since you first came into existence, but from which all humans seem to want to run away.

Love, Substantial Love, which is another name for God, has been the key to every mystery in your life to date. But now we come to a mystery which God, as God, can never know; hence, you may be lost as to the way to its solution. God is Life and thus He is the solution to our life and living. God is Love and thus He is the cause of all our love and loving. But God is not death — and yet toward death you have been moving steadily since the first moment God gave you life and made you a potential lover. What are you going to do about this mystery of death?

We all know we are going to die. But how many of us really believe it? We all know that each new heartbeat brings us nearer to our last one. Yet, how many of us actually believe that? What a baffling, bewildering mystery is the living, yet ever dying; the knowing, yet never knowing; the believing, yet unbelieving human being! We know, yet we do not know, that we are going to die. We believe, yet we do not fully believe, that we are going to know an end to earthly existence. We admit with our heads, but go on with our hands, our hearts, and our habits as if we had never admitted it with our heads. We are absolutely certain that we are going to die, yet we live on as if we were deathless. How account for such contradictoriness?

There is no human alive who, at one time or another, has not been conscious of his finiteness, his very real contingency, his palpably precarious and unpredictable existence. For everything about us, even the way we have to go about acquiring our loftiest and richest thoughts, manifests our poverty, our pain, our pitiable plight. Yet there is no person who has not within him a conviction that he is anything but a poor, weak, unimportant, and passing entity. How account for these self-canceling convictions?

By the very realization that we are not from ourselves, we come in contact with Reality. The clearer our concept of our own insufficiency, the stronger our consciousness of the Omnipresent One who is our Answer to our every deep perplexity. The deeper the analysis of self goes, the firmer becomes the conviction that we finite mortals are closely related to the Infinite and the Immortal. The more one watches men and studies their movements, the more clearly He sees God and that "gravitational pull" to God which is in every man. St. Augustine was as right to speak of that strong attraction every human being feels toward Him who is Being, as was Origen, when he said that the human soul is by its very nature Christian.

You have been sharing the insights of these two great Christian thinkers, and have seen how Revelation substantiates their every claim. For you have seen from Scripture that when God was creating man He already willed to make him a participant in Divine Life, and when re-creating him, this participation was to be made in and through Jesus Christ. Deeply rooted in every man is — a Christian. That is precisely why the mysteries in the life of Christ provide solutions for every mystery in the life of any Christian; for the life of every Christian, and of every man, is meant to be naught but a prolongation of that initial and eternal mystery which is Christ — the Incarnation. It follows then that man must die, yet never know death. For it is Christ who, in the Apocalypse, says: "I am the First and the Last and the Living One. I was dead, but how wonderful, I live forever and ever" (Ap 1:18). Every Christian is His member — every man is meant to be such — consequently, every man is going to die and live forever.

*Death* is as mysterious as life, if not more mysterious. It is not the end of life, nor the cessation of living. It cannot be defined as the absence of life. It appears to be all three, and, in a certain sense, it is all three. Yet, it is none of them. For man, once alive, never ceases living; man, once possessed of life, will never know its absence. The unchallengeable truth is that once man has come into life and begun to live, he will never know an end to living, nor a cessation of life. What, then, is this thing called death?

We describe it as the separation of the soul and body. That has become the classical description. But it is not a definition. We describe the mystery; we indicate the marvel-filled action; but we say not one word about what is specifically human in this action, nor do we describe what happens to *the man* in the mystery. It is *the man* who dies — not his body; most certainly not his soul. No. Something happens to the person, to the man as a whole. Better still, and much more accurate, is it to say that it is the person himself who dies.

It is seldom that you hear or read about the activity that is present in the death of a human being. Yet it is there. Man dies. Man does not merely suffer something passively. In dying, man does something: he acts. For death is not a biological fate against which man is utterly impotent; though this is the external aspect it exhibits, and the character which we usually conceive as the totality of death. But we are wrong. Death is an act — the act of the individual man who dies. It is a human act — an act of mind and will. Hence death is a living act; for it originates from within. It is a deliberate act inasmuch as it is a *self-affirmation* —

a free and the final one. In dying, and by his death, the individual's free, personal self-affirmation and self-realization achieves finality. This finality is intrinsic to death itself, and it is achieved by a spiritual, personal act of man.

That is neither new, nor should it sound strange. This is the traditional theological truth about that mystery we all must meet — and which should be met in a human manner. Death is something we should meet as rational animals. It is something we should meet as images of God, beings endowed with intellects and free wills. It is something we should meet as Christians, mystical members in the Body of Him who laid down His life. That is the crux — He laid it down; no man took it from Him. And we are His members! Therefore death should be for us what it was for Him — our final, free self-assertion and self-realization. We should act in death and not merely be acted upon. We will act, if we solve this mystery according to the truth God Himself has revealed to us. He died — He really was not "put to death." And we are His members.

In this approach we are dealing with reality — but that reality is a mystery. Incomprehensible it will remain, but it should never be unintelligible. We have been so accustomed to looking on death as something we must *undergo,* something that attacks us from without — and within, yet without our ever being in any way active in it, that we may have to plod a bit before we get our bearings.

Death has about it a manifest exteriority and a pronounced passivity. But there is also a marked interiority and a definite activity to it. Death is the consummation of the self from within; for it is that free and final self-assertion and self-realization mentioned above. Yet it is also submission to the destruction that comes from without. And there is a oneness to this twofold element; for the active and the passive, the exterior and interior, cannot be separated from one another without destroying the very essence of death.

It becomes less bewildering when we look at both elements individually. First, death is a personal consummation. The old tag about "As you live, so shall you die — and as you die, so shall you live eternally" has point right here. Death is an end to life on earth. It is an end to the union of the soul and body of the one who dies. By that very fact you can see it is a *consummation* of his *personal* life. That connotes an action *from within* by which this particular man brings the total result of his life's work to its final state. Now there has been, and there is, made a *deliberate* choice of this final state; for in each of his human acts during life man is enacting his death. This death is present in his deeds, those deeds that are deliberate, and in which he disposes of his whole person. Death is his final act, his final free choice, and the definitive consummation of all his other choices. Unquestionably, then, there is activity in death. Man dies.

But death is also something man suffers, something he undergoes. To it, then, there is a very definite passivity. That passivity takes us back to the beginning; for it means that, as universally experienced, death is a consequence of sin . . . of that original sin which we saw as making Eve both the world's first *Madonna* and the world's first *Pietà*. There is a causal connection between the death we will have to undergo and that first sin of our First Parents.

Death is a definite demonstration that man fell away from God, and lost that Divine Life given him at creation. In that demonstration lies implicitly the truth that, had Adam not listened to Eve, Cain would never have known any jealousy, let alone murderous anger; nor would Abel have ever known death. Before sin, man was not subject to death. You will understand that only if you remember that before sin man was in the state of grace; since grace is a gift, you can see that man never knew a purely natural state — he was always in the supernatural order. So we are not saying that death is not natural to man; we are only insisting that man has never been natural.

It seems necessary to insert that here, for there is an "ontology" to death, just as truly as there is a "theology." Some have tried to make them one by arguing from the fact that God Himself said: "Dust thou art, and unto dust thou shalt return" (Gn 3:19). God did say just that; but only after man had committed sin. It seems sounder theology (and, in the present economy, sounder ontology) to say that, had Adam not sinned, man would have known an end to his terrestrial existence, but that end would have come in a manner other than through the thing we now call death. He might have brought his personal earthly life to a perfect consummation by a pure, active self-affirmation, and thus experienced a "death without dying." But that is pure speculation. We are now dealing with reality. Death is a reality. We will probe it as far as we may.

The paradoxical elements in this phenomenon are the individual's self-possession — inasmuch as he makes a final and full self-assertion; yet, at the same time, the individual's complete dispossession of self — inasmuch as death brings on the dissolution of the composite which really makes the person a person.

But is death an end or a beginning? Both. For, since that promise made in the Garden to our mother according to the flesh has been fulfilled by our other Mother according to the spirit, and since He, of whom Abel was something of a symbol, has come and died the death, we must say that in our beginning was our end (for we were born to die, and began to die the moment we were born); and in our end will be our beginning (for we will begin to live really as the person, the being we actually are, only after we die.)

God became Man. As Man, God died. Death gripped Christ with its viselike grip, held Him in its darkness, in its ugliness, and with all its real relation to sin. But in Christ it became the contradiction of sin, the conquest of sin, and, consequently, a conquest of sin's consequence: death. Because Christ died, death, for every mortal man, is now birth. You go on living after death, and the life you will then live is the life of all living; for it is life with Him who *is* Life. Life with God is what death issues in. That is why the Church has her priests sing or say at every Mass for the Dead — *"Vita mutatur, non tollitur"* — "Life is changed. It is not taken away."

Since that is so, why is it that humans do not long for death? I know the usual answers. But do they answer? Here is the mystery: Each human has deep within him a dynamism that drives him on and on in the quest of more and more knowledge. Each has an insatiable hunger and an unquenchable thirst for love and ever more love. Within each is a veritable lust for life. None of these hungers, thirsts, or drives can ever be satisfied this side of the grave. It is not until we know as we are known; until we can love and be loved fully; until we have hold on a life that will never end and are free from every shadow of fear of dissolution, that we will be at peace with ourselves and at rest with our ever restless hearts. None of that can take place until after we have died. Yet, who longs to die?

There are moments of sincerity when we ask ourselves earnestly if we really believe what we profess to believe. This is one such. Every exile longs for a return to his homeland. Every prisoner craves release. Everyone in the valley of tears longs for the heights; all who sit in the shadow of death long for the sunshine that knows no such shadow. Legatees are always somewhat impatient to come into their inheritance. Sons, no matter how prodigal, long for the embrace of their father. And yet we have a Father. We have a Fatherland. We have a Father's inheritance. For we are "heirs, joint heirs with Christ." That means that the very Kingdom of God is *our* portion. And yet . . . do we believe what we profess to believe?

Paul presents us with a further test. He tells us that "this perishable nature of ours is destined to be clothed in imperishable glory, and this mortal nature of ours must be clothed in immortality." He adds that "when this perishable nature is clothed in imperishable glory, and this mortal nature is clothed in immortality, then will be realized the words of Scripture: 'Death is swallowed up in victory! O Death, where is your victory? O Death, where is your sting?' " (1 Cor 15:53–56.) And St. John goes lyrical and tells us what is to be: "How wonderful! God's dwelling place is among men; he shall make his home among them. They shall be his people, and God himself shall abide in their midst. He shall wipe away every tear from their eyes. No longer will there be death. No longer will there be mourning or cry of anguish or pain . . ." (Ap 21:3, 4). And yet we cling to life here in this valley of tears and sit quite content in the shadow of death! What a mystery is man!

Instead of longing for that which will enable them to know

perfect fulfillment on every level of their being, many men and women live their lives with a veritable phobia of this one thing that will enable them to be what they are made to. What is the basis of this very foolish fear? It can be granted that the fear of the unknown upsets most people. But we must be honest enough to see that it is a greedy grasp on the known that makes us cringe before the unknown. We know our friends on earth. We know our possession: our homes, our bank accounts, our stocks, our bonds. We know our sources of pleasure: the people, the places, the things that gratify our senses and, for a time at least, satisfy our appetites. We know the here and now. We cling to it. One need not have known luxury in life to cling with something like frenzy to life. The weariest of the weary and the poorest of the poor struggle to hold on to life when death comes on. Why?

If one's philosophy of life has been colored by the twentieth century's more common thought, one has been quite materialistic, hedonistic, and neopaganistic. For such, death is something to be actually hated. For to them it will be an end, and not a beginning; an end to everything they hold dear. It will be the dead end to the last blind alley of their lives. And, for them, there will be no turning back.

But even for the true Christian, there is a tinge of sorrow as death comes on that is both explicable and understandable. It means separation — and every separation is painful. The body will be separated from the soul; a member from the family; a citizen from the community. There will be loneliness for those who are left behind. None of us likes to be the cause of suffering, sorrow, or loneliness. So our hesitancy to welcome death which will bring all these into being among those we love is understandable. And yet the puzzle remains. Do we believe what we profess to believe? If so, why do we not long, as Paul did, "to depart and be with Christ"? It is, as he said "a lot far better" (Phil 1:23).

Earlier in this same letter Paul had compressed the whole philosophy of life and death for the Christian into a single sentence: "For me, to live means Christ, and to die, means gain" (Phil 1:21). The meaning of life is there: Christ. The purpose of living is there: Christ. The purpose of dying is there: to gain Christ.

We say we believe all that, and yet, how many of us long "to depart and be with Christ"?

Christ we know is with the Father in glory. Hence, for us to "depart and be with Christ" would most certainly mean "gain." It would mean going Home to the Father. The Germans have a beautiful name for death. They call it *heimgang,* "home-going." Heaven is Home for us — yet how many of us long to go Home? how many of us long with sincere, loving longing to be with our Father?

A story is told about an aged, holy abbot. When he died his monks, not only out of filial love for their spiritual father, but out of what they considered justice in the light of God's Revelation, felt certain that their holy old man had gone to Heaven immediately, had straightway joined the saints. They canonized him, as it were, privately. But one night, not long after his death, a holy old lay Brother had a vision. He saw his dead abbot in flames. In consternation and pity he called out: "Father, Father, what does this all mean? You — in Purgatory?" "Yes," came the reply, "and here I stay for the next forty years simply because, while in life, I did not long with sufficient ardor to 'depart and be with Christ.' I did not truly long for Heaven and the vision of God."

The God, who, in the Old Testament, begged: "My son, give me thy heart" (Prv 23:26); the God, who, in the New Testament, gave as summation of the Law: "Thou shalt love the Lord thy God with thy whole heart"; the God who is shown to us as a "jealous God" who would "not give His glory to another"; may well be the God who expects us, His children, to long to come Home, to yearn for a sight of Him, to crave to be with Christ, so that we might love the Father as He deserves to be loved by us, His sons. In other words, He may well expect us, while always obedient to His will, and ever awaiting His good pleasure, nevertheless, to yearn for death. And if we firmly believed what we profess to believe, wouldn't we so yearn?

Death, in its physiological manifestation, that is, in the subtle chemistry by which the soul is separated from the body, looks like an impenetrable mystery to us. God, the Author of life, alone knows exactly what this thing is that we call death. But we are not wrong when we see it as a summons from God, a call from the Creator. Hence, it can be an act of obedience on our part. That does not lessen the mystery of death itself or that of the chemistry of separation of soul and body. But it does give us something positive, and shows us that it is to be an act, and an act of a son of God. That brings us closer to the only solution we can reach. We have already seen that Christ is the Norm for all men. As this is true for all life, it is true for death. Christ showed us how to live. Christ also showed us how to end life on earth — and begin our glorious living. And once again we find Jesus Christ is the One Solution to our impenetrable mysteries.

Since it was our fallen nature that Christ assumed, He had to die. That was the sentence God had passed on human nature in the Garden. Death was the evidence that human nature no longer possessed that preternatural gift which Adam enjoyed before his sin. Death, then, was a manifestation of guilt inasmuch as it was a connatural expression of a situation brought about by sin. Christ accepted all that when He assumed our nature. Christ carried that sin and that guilt to Calvary. Christ died for us. Since then, in ultimate analysis, death has had no domination over any man — even though every man dies. This brings us to the heart of the mystery — and we will find it a loving heart!

As it can be said that, in assuming our fallen nature, Christ assumed our "life," and thus had to die in our stead, so it can be said that we, in and through Baptism, have assumed Christ's life-giving death, and, consequently, need never die. For sincere Christians the saying of St. Paul has literal truth: "I die daily." For this process of dying with Christ and thus winning new life in Christ permeates one's entire existence once he realizes he is Christ's member, and, consequently, "alive to God in Christ Jesus" (Rom 6:11). Daily the true Christian dies to his lower self, to sin, to the concupiscences, to the pride of life, to his many lusts — and dedicates and rededicates himself to God "as men who have come to life from the dead" (Rom 6:13). That commitment could not have been put more clearly than it was by St. Paul when he asked: "How shall we, who are dead to sin, still live in it? We know that our old self has been crucified with him, in order that the body enslaved to sin may be reduced to impotence, and we may no longer be slaves to sin; for he who is dead, is once for all quit of sin. But if we have died with Christ, we believe we shall also live with him. . . . The death he died was a death to sin once for all, but the life that he lives is a life for God" (Rom 6:2–10).

We died with Christ in the long ago. Christ will die with us when our hour comes. There is the mystery — and there its solution: we die and yet we do not die; we live, yet our living is a continual dying. To sharpen our focus we must stand beside the distraught Martha when Christ came to her four days after her brother's death and she said: "Master, if you had been here, my brother would not have died." Christ replies: "Your brother will rise again." It was comfort for Martha, but not too comforting at that precise moment, so she very honestly says to Christ: "I know he will rise again at the resurrection on the last day." Then Christ spoke those words that lighten our dark world with divine splendor: "I am the resurrection and the life. He who lives and believes in me, will live even if he dies; and no one who lives and believes in me shall be dead forever" (Jn 11:21–25).

Christ's death was life-giving. The death of any of His members can be the same. Christ's death was an act of obedience made precisely to wipe out that act of disobedience which brought death into being for us all. The death of any of Christ's members can be a similar act of obedience with somewhat similar effects.

Looking at Christ at His death and listening to His words, you will find magnificent self-assertion, splendid self-fulfillment, and manifestation of supreme self-possession. His *"Consummatum est!"* — "It is now completed!" is no cry of a defeated man. That is no surrender to superior forces. That is a strong man's strong assertion of his supremely strong self. Perfect self-possession is shown in His very depossession of Himself: "Father, into your hands I commit my spirit." St. Luke tells us Christ uttered these words in a "loud cry," and that "with that, he expired" (23:47). There is death. There is its activity and its passivity. But you will note that the activity is all but supreme. Christ laid down His life. No one took it from Him. Every dying Christian can look into the eyes of Death and tauntingly ask: "O Death, where is your victory?" No answer will come back from Death; for it has no victory: "Thanks be to God who gives us victory through our Lord Jesus Christ" (1 Cor 15:54–57).

Now the "portals of death" are not seen as something dark and dismal that will close down on life and leave all in stygian blackness, but rather as something that opens out and reveals to us vistas brilliant beyond all describing. Now the restless human mind can know peace, and the hungry human heart know its fill of joy; for the deepest longings of the human for what is true, what is good, what is beautiful, can be satisfied. For there, behind the portals will stand Infinite Truth, Infinite Goodness, Infinite Beauty, Eternal Bliss. Who would not long to "depart and be with Christ"?

How should a Christian die? He should let Christ take over and die in him. Death to too big and mysterious a thing for humans to face alone. That is why we were baptized. For that Sacrament made death in Christ possible just as it made life in Christ actual. We have nourished that life many ways, but most especially by the Eucharist — a Sacrament which gave us promise not only of death in Christ and as Christ, but also Resurrection to Glory with Him. So we have received a veritable vocation to die "in Christ Jesus" just as we did to live in Him. What is more, we have been called to die *as* Jesus Christ. We have been called to make this thing, toward which men move with such reluctancy yet inevitability, a holy and a hallowing thing, a sacred performance in which we will make our fullest self-assertion and attain our completest self-fulfillment as we obey our Father and give our spirit into His hands. Christ has shown us how. We have modeled on Him in life. We can model on Him in death.

But note well that it is not inevitable that we live and die that way. It is a matter of free choice — and strenuous effort. Good Friday, the first of all time, with its three human forms silhouetted on crosses against a blackening sky, teaches us that we must choose.

Of the three men only one died. Why was that? The thief on the right, Dismas as we have come to call him, cursed Jesus as much as the thief on the left, at first. But, as the hours wore on,

Dismas saw something in Christ's manner of dying that made his own death comprehensible to himself. He turned to the other thief: ". . . we suffer justly," he said, "and are getting what we have deserved for our crimes; but this man has done no wrong." Then he turned to Jesus and made the request that should be made by each of us a hundred times a day: "Jesus, remember me when you return in your glory" (Lk 23:41). You know the reply of Christ. We have no record concerning the other thief, but Scripture's silence makes us wonder.

It is now we die; for in dying to our sinful selves, we live to God in the sinless Christ. If we live that way to the end, we shall not die, we shall step through the door of death into eternal life. It will be all Cardinal Newman said it would be: stepping from shadows into the brilliant blaze of truth.

When Zeno, founder of the Stoic School of Greek philosophy, was once asked: "How shall I live?" he said: "Ask the dead." They, any one of them, whether they be in Hell, Purgatory, or Heaven, could teach us how to live. But we need not go to them; for we have been told how to live by Him who said: "I am the Vine, you, the branches." He is the Way. And for the answer to the question: "How shall I die?" we should reply: "Ask the *living*." That is what we have been doing in this chapter: we have been asking the living God how we are to die. His answer sounds very like the tag we referred to before: "As you live, so shall you die." If we live "in Christ Jesus," we shall die *as* Jesus Christ.

In our beginning was our end. Our real beginning was in Baptism. That Sacrament, by a law of nature, obligated us to live like Christ; for *agere sequitur esse* should have force in the supernatural realm as well as in the natural. We were given share in the nature of Christ at rebirth; our actions should have partaken of that nature and been revelatory of it in us. If we have lived like Christ, we shall die like Christ. As we, like Christ, commit our spirit at death into the hands of the Father, we can commend our dead bodies into the arms of Mary our Mother. Not physically, of course; for she is in Heaven, and we die on earth. But since in every *Hail Mary* we beg her to pray for us "now and at the hour of our death," we can make that petition mean that she be with us as she was with Christ — to share our sacrifice as she did that of her Firstborn, and aid us in making our deaths salvific, just as she collaborated with Him to make His redemptive. She will respond. Then, when we are taken from our cross of life by death, she will receive us into her arms — for Glory.

The Sorrowful Mysteries, which we share with Christ, will lead us as they led Him — to the Glorious.

*CHAPTER THIRTEEN*

# The Mystery That Sets You Aglow With God

*"If You Be Risen . . ."*

WE HAVE been back in the Garden of Eden often in this study, and have looked into the Book of Genesis again and again. It was essential. For there not only human life began — and human strife against God — but it was there too that God showed His loving mercy for us mortals by promising Christ. And if one thing has stood out in all this study it has been our intimate relations to God, our total dependence upon Him — and yet our fear-filling faculty that made our First Parents endeavor to be independent of Him, and has led us into the same insanity that we know as sin. We have moved in mystery from the first page, we shall continue to move in mystery to the last. We have entered the Mind and the Will of God — and found ourselves there "before the foundations of the world were laid." We know that when those foundations are shaken and time yields place to eternity we will still bespeak a relation to that Mind and Will. We have looked into eternity frequently, for we are eternal beings. Consequently, if there is one mystery that sums up our life it can be called the mystery of the "Pass-over"; for, to know ourselves, we have had pass over again and again, from time to eternity, from mortality to immortality, from corruption to incorruption, from sin to sanctity, from death to life, from humanity to divinity. So we should feel at home as we study the Paschal mystery and its vital significance for us. After looking into Genesis so often it will be stimulating now to look into Exodus; for if we found life in Genesis, it is in Exodus that our living is discovered; for the Red Sea is all around us — the Jordan is ever before us — the Promised Land beckons. The "Pass-over" is the all-embracing mystery — for us — for God — for the universe.

Paschaltide is the most exciting season of the year. It begins with a vigil that is all dark but which soon bursts out into the "light of Christ" which is the brilliance of the universe; for He is not only the "Light of the world," He is the Lamp of Heaven. The season then goes on with exciting apparitions of the risen Christ, takes us to the top of that mount at whose base He had agonized so that we can see Him ascend into Heaven; it ends with a Rain of Fire which is the Descent of the Holy Spirit who sets us aglow with God. The Paschal feast and the Paschal season prove to be the most personal of all the feasts and all the seasons of the year; for our entire lives are foundationed on the Pass-over, oriented to the Pass-over, centered in, fashioned by, and to be finished as a Pass-over. Hence, for us, Easter is the Feast of feasts, since it commemorates the Fact of all facts, as far as we are concerned.

Easter, as a feast, you have always known. But Easter, as a fact, is a different matter. Pius XII, by giving us back the Paschal Vigil, awakened us to the realization that few of us had probed into the mystery of the Pasch sufficiently. With that awakening came appreciation of the fact that here we uncover the foundation of our whole world and see on what our entire universe rests. St. Paul put this before us bluntly: "If Christ has not been raised, we are more to be pitied than all other men" (1 Cor 5:19).

"If Christ be not risen . . ." your life and mine, all our living has been based on illusion. We have been worse than dreamers walking in their sleep. We have been wide awake, but moving in delusion all our days. We have been deceived from the start; have lived in unreality every hour of existence, even as we became bruised and battered by the hard actualities that make up human living. We have not passed-over from any Egypt; we have not passed-through any Red Sea; but we have been in a desert all these years, tottering toward a mirage and not toward Living Water. Our lives have been worse than a masquerade; they have been sham, and we have been cruelly swindled. It has not been in mysteries that we have moved, but only in misery. For, "if Christ be not risen . . ." we have been robbed: for we have paid out all our lives — and nothing has been delivered to us; nothing can be. We have made total outlay of all we have and all we are — and have purchased nothing.

Paul gave another consequence that may sharpen our appreciation of the Paschal Fact. He said: "If Christ be not raised, you are still in your sins." We have seen something of the mystery of sin. We have seen its power. We have seen our First Parents expelled from Paradise because of it. We have seen mankind turned into a sorrowful "caravan on its way to death." We have seen the very Son of God put to death because of it. Sin ignited the eternal fires of Hell. "If Christ be not risen, we are still in our sins," still in that caravan that is on its way to that everlasting hopelessness and endless hate which is Hell. Theologically, if we are still in our sins, we are dead. "If Christ be not risen," we are lost forever!

Paul added another consequence when he said: "If Christ be not risen, your faith is groundless." Without faith man has no vision; and without vision men die. Without faith men should be glad to die; for there is nothing to live for! Without faith what choice have we? Either adoration or suicide have been the alternatives offered by the most thorough thinkers of the centuries. But if we are without faith whom can we adore?

Paul's condition is charged with potential enough for total destruction. But, thanks be to God, it is a contrary-to-fact condition. "Christ has been truly raised from the dead. He is the first fruits of those who have fallen asleep in death, because since man is the cause of death, so man is the cause of resurrection from the dead. Just as in Adam all men die, so too in Christ all men are brought to life" (1 Cor 15:20–22). Paul brings us back to those two corpses which marked the opening of what is really the story of your life. You are a son of Adam, who was born to become a son of God. You could never have become such, had not Christ risen from the dead. If Christ had not risen, then your life and mine, the life of every human, would indeed be what Macbeth called it: "a tale told by an idiot, full of sound and fury, signifying nothing."

The mystery in the life of Christ, which really solves all the other mysteries in His life, is this mystery of the Resurrection —

the Paschal mystery. And what is true of Christ and His life, is true of every Christian. Just as Christ was born to die and rise again; just as Christ was born to "pass-over" — so have you and I been reborn for the same pasch! The Resurrection is the climax of the Drama of Jesus Christ. We often say that we were redeemed by the Passion and Death of Jesus Christ. We were not! For "if Christ be not risen, we are still in our sins!" The Passion and Death were but prelude to the Resurrection — and without that Resurrection, the Passion and Death are without meaning. Paul awakens us to the theological reality that the Death and Resurrection of Christ are the two heartbeats of the Living Truth which is Christ — and in Him those of all Christians.

We will never know what life is all about unless we grasp the meaning of Easter, which holds in its heart the meaning of man. We have already seen that man, to be man, must be more than man. That was God's plan and purpose at both Creation and Re-creation. But man cannot be more than man unless He is in the God-Man; and no man can be there "if Christ be not risen. . . ."

Christ *had* to rise from the dead. He had placed the full burden of proof of His mission, his Messiahship, His Godhead, His One-ness with the Father, His very selfhood on this one fact — that He would rise from the dead. Demand after demand for proof of His claims were made on Him. What did He offer? — "The sign of Jonas." His people and their priests, the Scribes and Pharisees knew that sign well. Christ was determined that there would be no misinterpretation. He was most explicit about it: "A headstrong and adulterous nation demands proof of my claims. But a proof will not be given except the proof which Jonas gave: just as Jonas spent three days and three nights in the belly of the sea monster, so the Son of Man will spend three days and three nights in the heart of the earth" (Mt 12:39, 40). It was the same after He scourged the money changers out of the Temple. "What proof do you give us," they demanded furiously, "to show your right to do these things?" Christ gave them proof: "If you destroy this sanctuary, I will build it up again in three days." At the moment, the irate Jews did not catch the force of His proof. "Six and forty years this sanctuary was in the building; and you will build it up again in three days?" The very absurdity of the proposition, when stated that way, should have told them what St. John tells us: "He was speaking of the sanctuary of His body. After he had risen from the dead, his disciples remembered that he had said this . . ." (Jn 2:18–22). But it was not only His disciples who remembered. It was also the Jews. For, after His Death, they went to Pilate and asked for a guard. "Sir," they said, "we just remembered that when this imposter was still alive he said: 'In three days I shall rise again.' Please, therefore, give orders that the grave be made secure against violation until the third day; otherwise, his disciples might come and steal him, and then tell the people 'He is risen from the dead.' And thus the last imposture would be worse than the first" (Mt 27:63, 64).

He *had* to rise — or be proved a false prophet. He *had* to rise — to disprove the charge of being an impostor.

Had He been an impostor you can see what life would be like for you, for me, for everyman, by looking at the two disciples on the way to Emmaus the first Easter Sunday afternoon. Cleopas and his companion were two extremely dispirited men as they trudged along toward Emmaus as day moved toward twilight. They were disappointed men. They were men whose hopes had been blasted. When the Stranger joins them and asks what it is that they are discussing so seriously as they trudge along, Luke tells us the two disciples "stopped and sadness clouded their faces." Cleopas replies: "Are you the only visitor to Jerusalem that does not know what happened there these days?" With consummate artistry and acting Christ prods them: "Well, what?" He asks. These two disappointed men would only have been too anxious to pour out their hearts. They did just that; for St. Luke says they told "all about Jesus of Nazareth, who proved himself a prophet mighty in deed and word in the eyes of God and the mass of the people." But you can also hear heartbreak as they confess that "for our part *we had hoped* he might be the man destined to redeem Israel" (Lk 24:21).

Their vision of a redeemed Israel had been completely shattered by Friday's happenings. Without vision men die. These two disciples were really living dead men walking toward Emmaus. That is all any man could ever be: a living dead man walking toward some town that held nothing but other living dead men, had not Christ risen from the dead. The subtle irony of the entire scene tickles one. But there is more than that for our artistic sensibilities in this passage. He is a wise man who, Easter after Easter, walks to Emmaus. He will learn much about his God from his God — and learn very much about himself.

"O how dull you are!" says Christ, as Stranger, to these two downhearted disciples — and through them He says the same to many men of our own day. "How slow to understand when it comes to believing anything the prophets have said! Was it not necessary that the Messias should undergo these sufferings and thus enter into his glory?" (Lk 24:25, 26.)

That was a devastating question. The Jews failed to recognize Christ as Messias precisely because they were not looking for a suffering Messias. The connection between Christ's Passion and His glory is not causal, but it most assuredly is conditional. The sufferings He underwent did not produce His glory, but they were a necessary condition for His entrance into His glory. "Beginning with Moses" this Stranger went "right through the Prophets" and showed these two disciples that their Messias was "the suffering servant of Jahveh," hence, that it was *necessary* for the Christ to suffer as He did if He were to attain to His glory. That must have been one of the most delightful walks of all time, holding, as it did, the most absorbing conversation possible to men: the mystery of God's love for sinners!

Note that Christ's proof on the way to Emmaus is not that He was to rise from the dead, but that He was to rise from the dead in glory; not that He was to return to life, but that He was to return to them in His glorified life. That is of the utmost importance for us; for it is only the glorified Christ who is "vivifier" — only this Stranger on the road to Emmaus who can give us the life of all living — the kind He merited by His Passion and Death, and attained to by His Resurrection.

You could never call the week which stretches between Palm Sunday and Easter "Holy," had Christ not risen; for it would have been nothing but a week of horror. Nor would you be able to name the Friday in that week "Good," had not that following Sunday seen this Stranger alive and walking with the two toward Emmaus. Had not Jesus been able to appear to the Holy Women who hurried to the tomb that first Easter morning, then what they had witnessed Friday would not have been the "Sacrifice of the Mass" but the slaughter of a man. It is His rising from the dead that shows us His dying was sacrificial and His Death acceptable Sacrifice.

Sacrifice is making a gift to God. But since a gift is not a gift when it is offered, but only when it is accepted, there is ever so much more to sacrifice than mere oblation or offering. This proves how this Paschal mystery is the central point in our Religion and the focal point of our personal lives, and that *acceptance* is the all-important part of sacrifice.

Let us go back to Abel. He had done that which, in a way, brought on his death: he sacrificed to God. Going back to Cain, who has been one of the main characters in this book, we will find him doing something very similar to what his brother Abel had done. But we cannot say he is sacrificing to God. No, Cain *offered* to God. Genesis says: "Cain offered the fruits of the earth, gifts to the Lord." We know that "Abel also offered of the firstlings of his flock." There the similarity of the actions ends. For "the Lord had respect to Abel and his offerings. But to Cain and his offerings he had no respect" (Gn 4:3–5). In other words, God *accepted* Abel's offering and thus his firstlings became God's gifts — sacrifice. God did not accept Cain's offerings. So though offered as gifts to God they never became God's gifts; they never became sacrifice.

Nor will a "whole-burnt offering" do it. That adjective "whole-burnt" brings in a second element usually present in sacrifice and technically known as "mactation." That brings us to the "bloody sacrifices" which we find so prevalent among all peoples of the past. The victim was slain and offered, or offered and slain. The ritual was eloquent. The victim stood for the people who make offering to God. The slaying of the victim told God that this people would give their lives to Him. In symbolic language they were saying they loved God with all their hearts and would be His entirely. Impressive it certainly was — and is. But not even this slaughter (or "mactaction") coupled with that "oblation" (or offering) makes sacrifice. It always remains for God to accept — even in the case of "whole-burnt offerings" as we see in the First Book of Kings, where we read how Saul had been sent by God "to smite Amalec." God commanded that no one and nothing be spared. Saul was to "slay both man and woman, both child and suckling, ox and sheep, camel and ass." Saul smote Amalec, but "spared the best of the sheep and of the herds that they might be sacrificed to the Lord." At Galgal Saul "offered a holocaust to the Lord out of the choicest of the spoils he had brought from Amalec." Saul would sacrifice to God. He would make a "holocaust," that is, a "whole-burnt offering." His intention was good. But his obedience had been poor. God, through the mouth of His prophet, Samuel, told Saul that "obedience is better than sacrifice" — this kind of sacrifice which was "oblation" plus "mactation." — There had been offering and slaughter, but there was no sacrifice; for God did not *accept!*

To find genuine sacrifice we need to go to Mt. Carmel and witness that contest between Elias, the lone Prophet of God, and the four hundred priests of Baal. Each was to offer a holocaust to their God, and it was agreed "the God who shall answer by fire, let him be God" (3 Kgs 18:24). The priests of Baal received no answer to their pleas for acceptance. God answered Elias by sending fire which consumed his holocaust.

Fire from Heaven — that was the sign of *acceptation.* You see it in the Old Testament again and again. Fire from Heaven fell on the offerings of Abraham, Gideon, David, and Solomon. Fire from Heaven was the sign in the New Testament as well; for it was the Uncreated Fire of Divinity that came down with Christ's soul to the Body of the Victim that lay in the tomb after it had been *offered* in the Cenacle and *slain* on Calvary. In the supper room we had the *oblation.* On the Hill of Skulls we had the *mactation.* The Fire that fell on the Body in the tomb not to consume, but to inflame with the light and life of glory, was the sure sign of *acceptation*. After that sign, we can fall down as did the people on Mt. Carmel that day of Elias' triumph, and cry as did they: "The Lord, He is God!"

This is the mystery that enables us to see that "the Lord, He is God" — and the Lord God of the living. It is He who has set you and me alive with His own life — and aglow with His own glory.

It is scriptural truth that we are radiant with the very radiance that shone from the Christ of Easter. Paul tells us that the Christ, whom he calls the last (or second) Adam, "became a spirit imparting life." He became that only after the Resurrection. The only life He had to impart then was the life he was then living — the life of glory. "Being alive now," says St. Paul, "should no longer mean living with your own life, but with his life, who died for us and is risen again" (2 Cor 5:15).

St. Irenaeus wrote: "The living man is the glory of God." That does not mean that you and I live to *give* glory to God — though that is the first and the final purpose of our existence. The Saint meant that you and I, living now, *are* God's glory inasmuch as the risen Christ has become for us a "spirit imparting life" — His resurrected life, or that life which is glory.

Easter saw the birth of a new race of men: Christians. We live in the Christian era, that epoch issued in by the Resurrection of Christ. It is the era of the "new man" one who lives with a "newness of life," and who, in all truth, is a "new creature." Easter ushered in that epoch in which men are to live with the life of the risen Christ. By His Resurrection Christ "made all things new." This newness of life for man is manifested by "newness of spirit" and "newness of mind," which brings about a newness in morals and mores. The Jews of old lived by the Law of Sinai — the Mosaic Law. The Gentiles of old lived by the law of their conscience — the Natural Law. Ultimately both laws derived from God, and both were good. But Christ gave us the New Law. Under it we live. It is the Law of Love!

Unquestionably, in our day and age, these are "hard sayings" — and who could believe them? But before you walk away, listen to St. Paul: "Christ died for us all, so that being alive should no longer mean living with your own life, but with his life who died and is risen again . . . henceforward we do not think of anyone in a merely human fashion . . . for . . . when a man becomes a new creature in Christ, his old life has disappeared, everything has become new about him . . . we entreat you, in Christ's name, make your peace with God. Christ never knew sin, and God made him into sin for us, so that in him we might be turned into the holiness of God" (2 Cor 5:15 sqq., Knox trans.).

Can you question the fact that you are alive with God after that testimony? St. Ambrose, Doctor of the Church, did not doubt it. He taught his people of Milan to believe it with all their beings by bringing them back to Moses and the Burning Bush. "So speaks Our Lord," said the Saint to his Milanese. "In this church I appear to you as I once appeared in the thornbush. You are the thornbush. I am the fire. I am the fire in the thornbush of your flesh. I am the fire to illuminate you, to burn away the thorns of your sinfulness, to give you the favor of my grace" (*Epistola 63*).

The mystery of Easter is the mystery of your present moment. You are aflame with the Fire who is God — the God who came out of the grave. You glow with His glory, for you are alive to God in Christ, and Christ is living within you. Or as Paul put it, you should put it: "for me, Christ is life" (Phil 1:21).

Scriptural truths, far from solving the mysteries in your life, may seem to compound them. For in your honesty, you may say that, far from feeling aflame with the fire of God, you feel cold; far from feeling strong with the strength of the omnipotent God, you tremble with weaknesses; far from being radiant with the radiance of the risen Son of God, you feel that you are "of all man's clotted clay the dingiest clot." You may have reason for all these claims. But never forget the claim of St. Paul: "The Power of God reaches its perfection in weakness. . . . Gladly, therefore, will I boast of my infirmities, that the power of Christ may spread a sheltering cover over me. For this reason I take delight, for Christ's sake, in infirmities. . . . For when I am weak, then am I strong" (2 Cor 12:9, 10).

Such paradoxes sound foolish. They are foolish, but with that "foolishness of God which is wiser than the wisdom of men."

Paul insisted emphatically that God deliberately chose the "foolish," the "weak," the "ignoble and despicable" and "what counts for nought" . . . just so that he, who takes pride, must "take pride in the Lord" (1 Cor 1:26 sqq.). So you can glory in your weakness, but you can never doubt that you in your weakness are aglow with the glory of God.

God chose you out "in Jesus Christ" not because you were wise, but because you were foolish; not because you were strong, but because you were weak; not because you were good, but because you were sinful; not because you were saintly, but because "in Christ Jesus" and through Jesus Christ, who is the Glory of the Father, He could transform you into the holiness of God. This God, "who commanded light to shine out of darkness, has shone in our hearts, to give enlightenment concerning the knowledge of the glory of God, shining in the face of Christ Jesus" (2 Cor 4:6). That is the truth about you and your being. Yours are the lovely limbs, Gerard Manley Hopkins once spoke of, yours are the lovely eyes that Christ uses on earth this day. He is seen by the Father in the features of your face. God the Father looks on you and finds you alight with the loveliness of Christ, the risen Christ, the glorious God-Man. That is why St. Irenaeus could say "the living man is the glory of God."

Christ's Resurrection was a pledge of your own. When people hear they are to rise too many think only of that general resurrection when our corruption will put on incorruption. They seem to forget that we have already risen with Christ; that we are already alive with that life which in the New Testament is called eternal life! For that is the kind of life which the risen Christ communicates to the new race of men which came into being when He came out of the tomb afire with glory.

We know our merely human life is naught but a process of dying. We are not only threatened with destruction from without, but slowly decaying from within. That is what we see when we look at men merely as men. But when we look at the Man of all men, and in whom all men should "live, and move, and have their being"; when we look at this Man as He stands outside the tomb, we look upon a Man who has within Him the eternal life which He will share with all who become His members. So, within us, as surely as blood is within our veins, is this eternal life. Consequently, every baptized mortal is now alight with eternal flame.

Christ Himself said: "I tell you the plain truth: he who believes is in possession of eternal life" (Jn 6:47). He does not say "will receive eternal life" but *"is in possession of eternal life,"* Christ, Truth Incarnate, is talking about the present. He was even more specific about this glow of God within us when, after saving the woman taken in adultery from the death her captors seemed so anxious to mete out to her, Jesus "once more addressed them" as St. John says, and told them: "I am the light of the world. He who follows me will not walk in the dark, but have *the light of life"* (Jn 8:12).

St. John the Evangelist is very fond of three concepts relative to Christ: those of Light, of Life, and of Love. I need not tell you that these three are One — the One Son of God, the Man Jesus Christ. "Here is the message we have heard from him [Christ], and proclaim to you: God is Light, and in him there is not the faintest shadow of darkness. If we should say that we are united with him while we continue to shape our conduct in the atmosphere of darkness, we are liars; we fail to live up to the truth. But if we shape our conduct in the atmosphere of his light, as he himself is in light, we have union with one another . . ." (1 Jn 1:5-7). Through union with Him, of course. Hence, even though the age in which we live be dark, we can have light, walk in light, *be* light; for we have the Light of life within us. To be a Christian, then, is to be the light of the world; truly it means to be a *new man.* You are that man — thanks to Christ's Resurrection.

Of course it takes faith, theological faith. But that kind of faith is the very atmosphere in which the new race of men lives and breathes. It is very much like the atmosphere of Eden; for in it men walk with God, since theological faith is, as St. Thomas Aquinas teaches, a participation in the Divine Life. This gift of God "integrates us," says Thomas, "into Divine Knowledge." It locates us within God — in His Mind! There is where you find your real self; for you are a thought whom God is thinking. That is the existential reality. But once your eyes are opened by faith, you see yourself and know yourself to be just such a thought; consequently you come to consider all things with the very Mind of God — you see with His eyes! That is what makes you a new man. You have a new understanding of things, a new vision of reality, both the created reality and the Divine Uncreated Real. This new understanding is not understanding so much as it is wisdom.

*CHAPTER FOURTEEN*

# The Mystery of Your Future in the Present

~~~~~~~~~~~~~~~~~~~~~~~~~~~~~~~~~~~~~~~~~

*"He Raised Us Up and Enthroned Us . . ."*

WITH our contemporaries cringing in fear before the threat of destruction; with our civilization crumbling, as so many claim, as surely as did the civilization and culture of Rome; with the whole world in ferment as new nations emerge; and with a future filled with threats that are truly formidable, it seems absurd to speak of calm, contentment, peace of mind, and joy of heart. To some, no doubt, it will appear as if we were either ignorant of, or too cowardly to face, today's realities as we go on claiming to solve the mysteries of life by paralleling them with the mysteries in Christ's life. To speak of glory for each human being when the observant individual finds barbaric inhumanity on almost every side of him, and feels deep shame for his own kind; to speak of "walking in the light" when the world is so dark; to speak of the flame and the fire of love when hate is all about us, seems like giving the judicious just cause to grieve, the injudicious false grounds for hope, and the enemies of Religion reason to laugh and to say that it is "the opiate of the people."

Yet, precisely because we have taken the racing pulse of our times, we say with St. Paul: "Right now is the acceptable time! Right now is the day of salvation." *Because* we know what is going on, we are sure that right now is the time to realize that we have been redeemed; that we have been taken up into Christ; that we have already been made a sharer in the glory of God's own Son; that we can say with the same St. Paul: "ever at death's door, yet, wonder of wonders, we continue to live . . . as sorrowful yet always rejoicing, as beggars yet enriching many, as having nothing yet possessing everything" (2 Cor 6:2–10).

**163**

You must know *exactly* what is going on — and not to be duped by those who think they know, but who know only the appearances of reality. Your day and age has been called realistic. But more than one calm observer has wondered just how "realistic" it is. People tell you they want the "real." They insist that they want to face the "true." Hence, they demand that every mask be torn off, so that they can look upon the genuine no matter how nondescript, and see the actual no matter how disgusting. It is not a pose on their part. But it does stir pity on our part. For what else has ever been before them but the actual, the true, the real? Yet they have eyes and see not; ears and hear not; will not be still and learn! The "real" that they crave is Cain and his murder of Abel; but the more Real is Christ and His Redemption, not only of all such murderers, but also of their victims. The face that is true is one that bears the brand of Cain but which has the stigmata of Christ stamped over that brand, and all but hiding it. The mask that has been torn off, but which we carry in our hand, is that of Adam, the "old man," while the features we lift to the gaze of all are those alight with the glory of God.

The Christian who is conscious of his Christhood blinks no fact in this too human world of ours, but, by them, he is never dismayed, for he has eyes that see through these facts to the ultimate reality in them — and that he sees is divine. The fully conscious Christian is the true realist of the day; for he has grasped the Reality of all time — the risen Christ. With greater precision it might be said that the risen Christ has grasped him.

To the "children of light" — and that is what we humans have been called to be — our day is not dark; for we walk in the Light. Nor is it a day of slavery, despite the many slave states, and the "creeping Communism" in our own land; for we know the Truth, are in the Truth, and the Truth has made us free. Nor are we uneasy, restless, and confused, despite the almost universal unrest and confusion; for we know we are "in Christ Jesus" and that He is our Peace.

The reality that bears out Paul's paradoxes is ourselves: we, the *anowym* of the Chosen People of God, the little ones who are so great; the poor who are wealthy enough to enrich others;

the sorrowful ones who are always rejoicing; the dying who are ever bursting with life. How could we be otherwise when our Egypts are all left behind, our Red Seas, our desert wastes, our Rivers Jordan, have all been crossed. Yes, our Promised Land has already been reached — not by us personally, but by that Person in whom we live, and move, and have our being: Christ.

We individually toil away in our various Egypts, hurry through the walled-up waters of our different Red Seas, wander through our separate sandy wastes even as, in Christ Jesus, we now sit at the right hand of the Father. Our Moses strikes no rock to bring out water; He is both the Rock and the Fountain of Living Water. Our Moses climbs no Sinai to talk with God; He is God, and He talks with us. Our Moses need not ask to see God's glory; for He is that Glory, and He shares it with us. All of which shows not only that we are living in paradox but that we are living paradoxes. But we are never confused; for we are clear about, and conscious of, the one Great Reality — the Risen Christ. Nor are we ever unmindful of the one world-transforming fact: He is in us on earth, and we are in Him in Heaven. We live our future in the present.

All this takes careful thought and deep faith. But we can thank God that we are being aided in both our thought and our belief in this mid-twentieth century by such simple and symbolic things as the final Station in the Way of the Cross — the Fifteenth, not the Fourteenth. Years back this Way ended with the burial of Christ. But to have it end there was to truncate truth. God did not become man in order to die. Not even in order to die, be buried, and rise again. God became man to be glorified. Christ himself told us this. On the first Palm Sunday He explicitly said: "Come at last is the hour for the Son of Man to be glorified" (Jn 12:23). His glorification came not by His Resurrection alone, but by His Resurrection, Ascension, and Enthronement at the right of the Father. The Fifteenth Station intimates all this as it shows the glorified Christ outside the empty tomb. But the point is that Christ is the "last Adam," who "rose for our justification"; and He who was thus glorified, because He is the "last Adam," gives us what God, in the Old Testament, "would not give to another" — a share in

His glory. In Baptism we not only rose with Christ, we were robed in His glory.

Paul puts our life story in a paragraph which begins: "Once you were dead by reason of your transgressions and sins. . . ." That statement is irrefutably true of any and every human, even the most sinless; for, with but one exception, we were all born in sin. Hence, we were dead. "But God, who is rich in mercy, was moved by the intense love with which he loved us, and when we were dead by reason of our transgressions, he made us live *with the life of Christ*." Paul goes on: "Together with Christ Jesus and in him, he *raised us up,* and *enthroned us* in the heavenly realm" (Eph 2:1–6).

Three mysteries in the life of Christ are so interlinked that they form one complete action: His Resurrection led to His Ascension, and His Ascension called for His Enthronement at the right of the Father. What is true of Christ is true of Christians, as is evidenced by the excerpt above. So again I say your future is in your present; for Paul says you have been "raised up in Christ," and in Him you have been "enthroned in the heavenly realm."

Who can understand that? Who can take such statements as true? Only the wise! If we were in Paradise with Adam — and we most certainly were — what is to prevent us from being in Heaven with Christ? It is as simple as that. Adam lost us the first Paradise; Christ regained for us the real Paradise, the eternal one, which is Home.

We, pragmatic Americans, find difficulty in taking such truths to ourselves and making them part of our everyday living. We know all too well that, physically, we are on earth — and far from Heaven and Home. But there precisely is the fault with much of our living. It is altogether too physical, which, in ultimate analysis, is not the human part of us at all. It is not the body that makes us men; it is the mind. "We are what our thoughts are." So we must convince ourselves that our minds, which means our imagination, intellect, and will, can lift us above earth, above the body, above time, and allow us to live "in Christ, with Christ, and through Christ." Consequently, the theological truth about our "ascension and enthronement" can be made truly vital for us.

Our Liturgy upon earth is really the Liturgy of Heaven; for the One Liturgist in Heaven and on earth is Christ Jesus — the risen, ascended, and enthroned Victim of Calvary. Hence, when we offer Mass we are cooperating with Him in the re-presentation of that complete unity that is Good Friday, Easter Sunday, Ascension Thursday, and the Enthronement.

One hesitates to labor a truth, lest he belabor it. But this present truth is so vitally important that the hazard is well worth running. The mystery of Christ, as well as the mystery of Christians, is the Paschal mystery — the Passover, or, as some are calling it now, "the breakthrough." But we must view this mystery as a unity. We celebrate three separate feasts (if you will call Good Friday by that name). We have Good Friday, Easter Sunday, and Ascension Thursday. Historically, there were three separate occurrences: Christ died on Friday; He arose on Sunday; He ascended visibly on Thursday. Theologically, however, we are dealing with one dogma — that of Redemption; with one fact — that of the glorification of the human nature assumed by the Word. Looked at theologically, then, these occurrences are one continuous act in three phases: Christ empties Himself on Calvary and, on that same day, His "emptied-out Corpse" is buried; on the third day that emptied-out Corpse is filled again, but this time with the very Glory of God; the final phase is enacted when this glorified Christ takes His place at the right hand of the Majesty of God. Christ's Passion and Death were the necessary antecedents to His consequent Resurrection, Ascension, and Enthronement. Our sins had to be wiped out. Calvary did that. But we had to be brought to life again after that wiping out. Christ "rose for our justification." But that word "rose" means not only Resurrection, but also Ascension and Enthronement; for it is only the ascended and enthroned Christ who is "Vivifier."

Paul has expressed all this in his Epistle to the Hebrews. But perhaps we can simplify and clarify the whole matter by concentrating on one aspect: Priesthood — Christ's and your own.

Christ was Priest from the first moment of His Incarnation. But, following now the theory of Maurice de la Taille, we see that Christ exercised His Priesthood liturgically and officially when, in the Cenacle on Holy Thursday evening, He "took bread into his hands and, after saying grace, broke it into portions, which he gave to the disciples with the words: 'Take! Eat! This is my body.' He also took a cup and, after saying grace, passed it on to them with the words: 'Drink of it, every one of you; for this is my covenant-blood, which is about to be shed for the sake of many, with a view to forgiveness of sins . . .' " (Mt 26:26–28). That priestly act, technically known as *oblation,* led Christ on to what is called *mactation,* which means slaughtering. Christ is not only the New Law's only Priest; He is the New Law's only Victim. So His priesthood, exercised in the Cenacle on Thursday night, led Him on to the exercise of His Victimhood on Calvary the next day. *Acceptance* was given on Easter Sunday morning when Christ rose, ascended, and was enthroned. But do not think for a moment that He was enthroned just to sit there next to Divine Majesty. No. Paul tells you He is there exercising His Priesthood through that Blood of His which "speaks more eloquently than Abel's" (Heb 12:24).

Again we are faced with the corpse with which this book opened. But we are now far along in the solving of the mysteries of your life. We not only meet Abel in this Epistle to the Hebrews, but we meet him and his sacrifice every day in the Sacrifice of the Mass. For, after the Consecration, when we have the Christ who rose, ascended, and was enthroned on our altars as the Victim of our Sacrifice, we pray to God to "look upon our offering with a favorable and a friendly eye, and to accept it with the same pleasure wherewith He accepted the offerings of Abel."

Have you ever asked yourself what you meant by that request? If so, have you ever fully answered your own question? It does seem like a strange request. For, at the Offertory of your Mass, with and through your official representative, the priest at the altar, you asked the Trinity to accept the oblation you were making "in memory of the Passion, Resurrection, and Ascension of our Lord, Jesus Christ." The officiating priest then went on and, in the Person of Jesus Christ, did again exactly what Christ did in the Cenacle. He took bread, blessed it, bent over it, and whispered those transubstantiating words: "This is My Body." Over the chalice of wine he bent and whispered: "This is My Blood." After those sacred words the Christ on your altar was different from the Christ in the Cenacle. For on the altar you had the glorified Jesus Christ — the Victim who was Victor over death, sin, and the devil. On your altar was the Christ who sits at the right hand of the Father. In all actuality it was He who offered and consecrated the wheat and the wine through the person of your officiating and consecrating priest. The same Jesus, but His manner of offering in the Mass is different from His manner of offering in the Cenacle, and His state of Victimhood is different in the Mass from what it was on Calvary; for it is the glorified Christ, the ascended and enthroned Christ, who offers "the Sacrifice of Calvary," which is now the Celestial Sacrifice — and your Mass and mine.

Does it not seem absurd to ask God to accept our Offering as He did the offering of Abel when we know the Blood of Christ "speaks more eloquently than the blood of Abel"? What is more, we have just told God, after the Consecration, that we were calling to mind the "blessed Passion, Resurrection and glorious Ascension of our Lord Jesus Christ" and were offering Him a "pure Victim, a holy Victim, a stainless Victim" who was none other than the Christ who sits at His side. Why should we ask Him to accept One He has already accepted and enthroned? The reason is that in Mass Jesus Christ, the eternally Glorified One, is not alone. You are in Him, so am I. So is every member of His Mystical Body. We, too, are priests and victims in Mass. So there is a profoundly legitimate reason for pleading with God to accept our offering. We, who are brothers to Abel and Christ, are also brothers to Cain; and, as yet, there is no finality to our state or ultimate relationship. We have already "passed over" and "broken through" in the Person of Christ, and are seated in glory in Him, but, as yet, we have not personally "passed over" or "broken through." Hence we can yet show earth and Heaven that we are more like Cain than Christ. The One and Only who can keep us from being Cain — and being like him for eternity — is the risen Christ. The one way in which He will do it is through communication of His grace, which is the "seed of glory." Without Him we can do nothing. But with Him there is nothing we cannot do.

"Breakthrough" describes Christ's redemptive act very vividly, for Christ, by His Passion, Death, Resurrection, Ascension, and Enthronement, broke through the lines of sin, the battlements of Satan, and even the "hid battlements of eternity" and death. Christ broke through to Heaven, eternal life, and endless glory. "In Him" you and I shared in the "breakthrough."

Paul describes this breakthrough to glory thus: "He humbled himself and became obedient to death; yes, to death on a cross. *That is why* God has exalted him and given him a name that is above all names, so that at the name of Jesus everyone in heaven, on earth, and beneath the earth should bend the knee and should publicly acknowledge to the glory of God the Father that Jesus Christ is Lord" (Phil 2:7–11). The phrase "that is why" shows the intrinsic connection between Good Friday, Easter Sunday, and Ascension Thursday. It was not that God had promised to glorify Christ if He suffered and died, but that God, by His very Nature, and by the very nature of Christ's redemptive act, is constrained to glorify Him. In other words, glorification is contained in the Passion and Death as the flowered lily is contained in the bulb.

Note the personal meaning in all this for you. Christ "broke through" to a *newness of life.* His Resurrection was not at all like His recalling to life of the son of the widow of Naim, the daughter of Jairus, or Lazarus. At His command they came back to the same kind of life they had left at death — human life. Further, they came back to life only to die again. The Christ, however, "broke through" from a form of life that was subject to death, to another form of life that was conqueror of death. He "broke through" from a life in which there was sin; in fact God "made Him sin" while in that kind of life. But the life he "broke through" to is a life in which there is no sin. "We know that Christ, having risen from the dead, will die no more; death shall no longer have dominion over him. The death that he died was a death to sin once for all, but the life that he lives is a life for God. Thus you too must consider yourselves as dead to sin, but alive to God in Christ Jesus" (Rom 6:9–11).

The dynamic phrase there is "alive to God in Christ Jesus." Paul is telling you that you have been engrafted, as it were, on this risen and glorified Christ. Consequently, just as the graft lives by the life of the tree into which it has been engrafted, so you live to God with the very life of Christ. "We were buried in death with Him by means of Baptism, *in order that,* just as Christ was raised from the dead . . . so we also may conduct ourselves by a new principle of life" (Rom 6:4). That new principle is the Christ-principle; that new life is the life of the glorified Christ. He it is who gives you the ability to "breakthrough" to eternal glory.

You can make that "breakthrough" now! You can make it any hour of the day or night. You should be making it three hundred thousand and more times a day. For you can unite yourself with Him who has already broken through as He is offered again and again in Mass "from the rising of the sun to the going down of the same." Indeed Paul gives us reason to rejoice, as he tells us that "we have confident access to the Holy Place, thanks to the blood of Jesus, by following the new and living path which he has opened for us through the veil . . ." (Heb 10:19–21).

It takes faith. But faith is the breath of life. The man without faith is a dead man, no matter how active he may appear. The just man, we know — and he alone merits the name of man — lives by faith. Paul was explicit: "Faith is the foundation of the blessings for which we hope, the proof of the realities we do not see. . . . By faith we understand that the world was fashioned by God's word in such a way that what is visible has an invisible cause. By faith Abel offered to God a sacrifice richer than Cain's. Through that faith he received testimony that he was holy, since God bore testimony in favor of his gifts. And through his faith, dead though he is, he still speaks" (Heb 11:1–4).

Abel has been speaking to you from the opening of this book. He speaks now in a special manner as he tells precisely what you need, and what your world lacks: *faith.* Earlier you saw how desperately the men of our times need hope. Now you must realize that the foundation of all hope is what Paul speaks of, and Abel makes manifest: faith. Faith gives you the eyes of God so that you can see the invisible. But those invisible realities are the only true ones — and the ones so many moderns miss. It is estimated that only 18 percent of humans living in our world today believe in God. One out of five humans knows his own Father. Only one out of five knows why he is alive. Pitiable indeed is the state of modern man! But all the more reason for us to heed Paul and "eagerly throw ourselves into the struggle before us, and persevere, with our gaze fixed on Jesus" (Heb 12:2).

Your attention has been called more than once to the truth that the thinking man has but one choice to make: either suicide or adoration. That may have struck you as extreme. But to show you how accurate it is, let me give you some facts and figures. Facing both will prove to you that the only solution to the mysteries in your life are these mysteries in the life of Christ.

The Middle Ages had their quota of wrongs. But they have been rightly called the Ages of Faith. Many more than 18 percent of the inhabitants of the globe in those days believed! They believed in God — in man — and in the God-Man. That gave them hope. That also gave them love for life. Consequently, in those days, suicide was practically unknown. After the Renaissance, with its rebirth of pagan ideas and pagan practices, with consequent loss of faith, the suicide rate went up very markedly. From the time of the Protestant Revolt in the sixteenth century, the suicide rate is appalling.

What's wrong with our world? The answer is simple! — Not enough people are "in Christ Jesus" — are letting themselves be guided by love as Christ loved us. One out of every three humans lives under direct domination of atheistic Communism. Only one out of five humans believes in God. And here in our United States there are one million professed atheists. Small wonder there is so little joy in our world!

Hilaire Belloc once pointed out that our boastful and often noisily optimistic century has been definitely marked by a rising tide of despair. That rising tide is easily accounted for in the truths you have been learning about the relation of hope to faith. We are well past the mid-century mark. The tide of despair continues to rise; for more and more of our contemporaries are losing faith in God, and all faith in man. Where lies salvation? Take the word of God the Holy Spirit as He speaks through St. Paul: "He [Christ], because he continues forever, has an imperishable priesthood. Consequently he is able at all times to save those who come to God through him, living always, as he does, to make intercession on their behalf" (Heb 7:25).

That last will answer a question that may have arisen in your mind about Christ during the forty days that intervened between His Resurrection and His Ascension. Where was He? What kind of a life did He lead? What was he doing when He was not appearing to His Apostles, disciples, and friends? He was in Heaven doing then what He is doing now. For there were two modes and two moments to Christ's Ascension: the invisible, but real, one by which He went to take His seat by the Father's side on the very day of His Resurrection, and the visible one, which took place before His disciples from the top of Mt. Olivet forty days after the first Easter. We usually think only of this latter one. But the former was the more important; for it crowned Christ's Resurrection and His whole earthly life; it accounts for the manner of His appearances during the forty days, and shows us many of the qualities of the glorified Body. Christ was in glory from the moment of His Resurrection and was doing what Paul says: He was there at the Father's side as Eternal Theotyte, that is, as Accepted Sacrificial Victim — who leads a life that is one incessant pleading with the Father for our salvation.

How does He plead? — With His Blood. With His glorified Humanity, scarred as it is with those five wounds, vivid marks of the "breakthrough" of His love for us. The effects of that eternal pleading is poured out to us in time through Mass, the Sacraments, and His Spirit who "broods over the bent world."

Now you are in position to understand why, in Mass, we speak of the Passion as *beata* — which means, ultimately, "blissfully happy." Of course we do not mean to call the betrayal by Judas, that Agony in the Garden, those utterly illegal trials, the night in the dungeon, the scourging at the pillar, the crowning with thorns, the way of the cross, the crucifixion, and the death itself "blissfully happy." Yet, there, in the middle of Mass, stand the words: *beata passio*. Our Liturgy was composed with meticulous care — every word scrupulously weighed before being accepted. So the *beata* attached to *passio* means that we must take the redemptive act in its entirety. It began, if you will, in the Cenacle Thursday night; it can be considered ended, in one sense, Thursday noon — the Thursday of the Ascension which brought on the Enthronement. Since the *passio* led to that "breakthrough" it is rightly called *beata*.

That *beata passio*, in its fullness, with its "breakthrough" and all its glory is yours in every Mass. For Christ is yours. What is more, you are Christ's. Hence, your great work in the world is to be a witness to Christ, a living witness who, by your way of living, tells the world that Jesus Christ is alive and in glory. That kind of witnessing will depend on your faith. But if that faith is lively, you will be full of hope, and aflame with love. Once you are that alive to God you will be able to say with St. Paul: "I count everything loss in comparison with the supreme advantage of knowing Christ Jesus, my Lord. For his sake I have suffered the loss of all things, and I count them as rubbish that I may gain Christ, and be found united to him, not with a holiness of my own derived from the Law, but with that which is obtained by faith in Christ, the holiness which God imparts on condition of faith. I would know Christ and what his resurrection can do. I would also share his sufferings, in the hope that, if I resemble him in death, I may somehow attain to the resurrection from the dead. Not that I have already attained this ideal, or have already been made perfect, but I press on, hoping that I may lay hold of it, since Christ has laid hold of me. Brothers, I do not consider that I have reached it. But one thing I do: forgetting what is past, I strain toward what is ahead. With my eyes fixed on the goal, I press on to the prize in store for those who have received from above God's call in Christ Jesus" (Phil 3:8–14).

You have received that call. That, really, is the mystery of your life. It remains for you to fix your eyes on the goal, forget the past, and strain toward what is ahead — strain toward that future of yours which is already present. Do so with the same confidence Paul displays in the foregoing lines; for you cannot fail to arrive where Paul arrived, where Jesus Himself arrived, if you will but allow the Spirit to fill you with His fire.

Now for realism in sheerest form: you, weak and wayward as

you are, in your metaphysical reality are naught but a "capacity for God." Hence, you will never be yourself until your capacity is filled with God. That means that into your weakness His strength must be poured; into your darkness His light must stab and fill every nook and cranny with His shining; into your deadness must come His life — the life He now lives. Then you must walk out into your world and *be* witness that He has risen, ascended, been enthroned.

I need not give any directive for your witnessing. Christ Himself has specified the whole regime: "If anyone wants to be my follower, he must renounce himself and shoulder his cross; then he may be a follower of mine. Why, he who would save his life shall lose it; but he who freely parts with his life for the sake of the gospel will save it in the end. Clearly, what does it profit a man to gain the whole world when his life is forfeited in any case? Or what price can man pay down to purchase life forever? Furthermore; if one is ashamed of me and my message before this adulterous and sinful race, of him the Son of Man will, in turn, be ashamed when he returns wrapt in his Father's glory and escorted by his angels" (Mk 8:34–38).

To many modern ears that will be a "hard saying" — and many will actually ask: "Who can hear it?" The answer is plain: Those who love! Those who go through life on earth burning with God, who is within them, and for God, who is about them.

# CHAPTER FIFTEEN

# The Mystery of Flame That Is in Your Life

## *". . . Tongues Like Fire . . ."*

A CHILD of three or four years can tell that light, life, and love *are*. But no philosopher of three or four aeons can tell us *what* they are. It is an amusing — and often an irritating — fact that the simplest and best known things are the very things we cannot ultimately analyze nor adequately define.

Life and death are all about us, so are darkness and light, and who is there who has not experienced some love — and known at least the stirrings of love's opposite. But who can tell just what life is, or light, or love? Yet St. John's Gospel and Epistles treat of almost nothing else. Even his visions in the Apocalypse are flooded with his three favorite themes. What is even more pertinent and personal to each of us is the fact that God's Word Incarnate used these three words not only about Himself, but also about His followers. "I am come that they may have *life*. . . . Just as the Father is the source of life, so, too, has he given the Son the power to be the source of *life*. . . . He who believes in the Son possesses eternal *life*." A dozen other texts could be cited as they fell from the lips of Jesus telling about life. The same is true regarding *light*. John opens his Prologue by telling how the Word was life, and that this life was the *light* of men; how this *light* shone in the darkness; and how He was the true *light* that illumines every man. Later John has Jesus saying to a hostile crowd of Pharisees: "I am the *Light* of the world. . . ." Then, just before His Passion, we hear Christ crying out: "I have come into the world as a *light,* so that no one who believes in me might remain in darkness." As for love, it was John who gave us the

178

definition: "God is *Love*." If we but scan the discourse at the Last Supper we will find John depicting Christ with the word *love* on His lips almost incessantly.

Since life, light, and love so filled the Mind, Heart, and whole Being of Christ, so must they fill those of Christians; for just as these three mysterious entities were the very Being of the Word Incarnate, so must they be that of those who have been so incorporated into Him that they carry on that Incarnation. The call to be a Christian is not a call to imitate Christ, nor a summons to follow Christ, but a veritable command to *be* Christ. He was Life, Light, and Love. You must be the same, or dare not call yourself a Christian.

Impossible? It has been already accomplished — at least in an inchoate form. Baptism made you a "new creature," gave you a "new principle of life," and thus enabled you to "walk in newness of life." All that "newness" came from the Ancient of Days — from Christ, through His Spirit. (You were "born again of the water and the Spirit.")

Now you are in the depths of the Mystery of mysteries — that of the Trinity. For the facts revealed force us to focus on the processions that took place in the Trinity: that of the Son from the Father, and that of the Holy Spirit from the Father and the Son. For the possession of Life, Light, and Love bespeak the missions of the members of the Trinity, and those missions bespeak relations to those processions.

Whenever you recite the Creed, you speak these truths: for you tell how you believe in the Father, and think of Him as the Creator and Provider, the Principle whence all proceeds; you tell of your belief in the Son, who proceeded from the Father, and was missioned to earth to redeem you; you tell of your belief in the Spirit, of His procession from the Father and the Son, and His mission by both to sanctify you.

You profess belief in the fact that only the Son and the Spirit have been sent on missions; you conclude that only those in the Trinity who have known procession can be sent on missions. The Father has never been sent; for the Father never proceeded. He is the Principle from whom the Son was generated. From Father and Son, as from one Principle, came the Holy Spirit. These facts show you the life of the Trinity is a life of light and love — intellect and will. Because they know perfectly and love perfectly, They live a life that is bliss. That you might one day have a share in that bliss-filled life God sent His only Son on that mission we call Redemption. Once He had completed His mission, the Son went back to the Father and with Him sent the Holy Spirit on another mystery-filled mission which is the one now being fulfilled by Him in you — the mystery of sanctification that leads to salvation.

Neither of those missions will mean what they should to you until you realize that both of them concern you personally. Paul said of Christ: "He loved *me,* and gave himself up *for me*" (Gal 2:20). You can say the same; for Christ was sent for *you;* and He and the Father sent the Holy Spirit to *you.* Never forget that God's thought of you is personal; God's love for you is the same. God never thinks of you as one in the mass of humanity. He thinks of you as one. Thinking of you as one, He loves you just as if you were the "one alone."

The personal element is the important element. For while it is true that you were born into a social unit, the first and final truth is that you are a person. As a person you were born. As a person you will be sanctified and saved — or not sanctified and damned. Hence, when we come to absolutes and ultimates, there is a certain form of selfishness that is highly salutary — and necessary. For you, as you, must realize your relations to God. You, as you, must care for your soul. You will do that only if you, as you, live the life you know God would have you live. That, of course, will take in countless social relations and community complexities; nevertheless, it will be to you, this lone individual person, this unique and isolated one that is you, that responsibility will come home. Consequently, it will be by this "one alone" who is you, that answer will have to be given to the only true "One Alone." You must be selfish enough to look to your own sanctification and your own salvation, for, just as you have but one life to live, so you have but one soul to save — your own life, and your own soul. That is a frightening responsibility. No one could carry it if he did not believe with Paul: "He [Christ] loved *me,* and gave himself up *for me*" (Gal 2:20). For that connotes the correlative truth which can be stated thus: "He loved *me,* and sent His Holy Spirit, the Spirit of Love and Truth, *to me.*"

If you read the final discourse Christ gave at the Last Supper you will learn how preoccupied He was with this mission of the Holy Spirit. It is not His Passion, or even His Resurrection, Ascension, and Glorification that takes His attention so much as the sending of the Holy Spirit. He told the Apostles again and again that He was going to leave them, but in the next breath He always added a consoling truth. For instance, "I am now about to go — for the very purpose of preparing a place for you" (Jn 14:3); and again: "I am going home to the Father — and should you ask anything in my name, I will do it" (Jn 14:13); then there is that "Do not let your heart be troubled! Do not let your heart despair! — You have heard me say: 'I am going home and I am coming back again'" (Jn 14:28). But the more insistent message was about the mission of the Holy Spirit. "I will ask the Father, and He will grant you another Advocate to be with you for all time to come, the Spirit of Truth" (Jn 14:16). Then, even more strongly: "When the Advocate whom I am going to send you with a mission from the Father — the Spirit of Truth who proceeds from the Father — has come, he will witness on my behalf" (Jn 15:26). Finally: "I tell you the truth: it is to your advantage that I depart. Unless I depart the Advocate will not come to you; whereas, if I depart, I will send him to you. . . . There is still much that I might say to you; but you are not strong enough to bear it at present. But when He, the Spirit of Truth, has come, he will conduct you through the whole range of truth" (Jn 16:7–13).

This earnestness on the part of Christ concerning the mission of the Holy Spirit tells the thoughtful reader that a period of transition was ending as a new pact between God and His people was coming into being. The Old Covenant was ended. A New Covenant was to be made. Paul tells us that "Christ was the mediator of this more excellent covenant" and that it was based on "more excellent promises." He gives those promises verbatim as he cites the Prophet Jeremias: "See, days are coming, says the Lord, when I will conclude a new covenant with the house of Israel and with the house of Juda, not like the covenant I made with their fathers the day I took them by the hand to lead them out of the land of Egypt . . ." (Heb 8:8).

There you have clear reference to what can be called the first mode of God's love. It is that of a father. It was manifest from the time of Eden to the Incarnation. We can attribute it to the Father, for it is a paternal love. It is the love that gives *life* — and preserves it. It is a patient love — that of the father of the prodigal, waiting for the son to have done with the "husks the swine did eat." God was a Father to the entire human race, but very especially to His Chosen People. He made a covenant with them. To it He was faithful, even though they, as a whole people, very seldom were.

Then came Christ — and a new mode of love was manifest by God for His human beings. This was the love that gave *light;* for Christ came as the "Light of the world" sent precisely to "enlighten all men who were in the world." He came not to end the love of the Father of the Old Testament so manifest in Providence, the Prophets, the Law, and the Pact. Christ came to fulfill the Law and the Prophets as He Himself said: "It is not my mission to annul, but to bring to perfection. I assure you emphatically: before heaven and earth pass away, not a single letter or one small detail will be erased from the Law — no, not until all is accomplished" (Mt 5:18). The Light of the world went out when Christ cried: "It is now accomplished" (Jn 19:30). The prophecies had been fulfilled; the Law brought to perfection. Mankind was now ready for God's third mode of love — the kind that is *love*.

You have been studying the progress of the love of God for His human creatures from the moment you looked upon the world's first corpse. Abel, the first man to earn "the wages of sin," was dead. You saw him in the arms of his mother — and yours — Eve, the first sinner. But it was in her presence, after that first sin, that you heard the first "annunciation" of the Redeemer and the promise of triumph over Satan and sin. That promise was fulfilled when the other Corpse was taken from the Cross, placed in His Mother's arms: giving us the world's most fruitful *Pietà* — she, a sinless Mother — who is your Mother — holding Her sinless Son — who is your God.

But note the progress of God's love. For millennia on millennia He had loved the children of Eve, the brothers and sisters of Cain and Abel, with a merciful love; a love whose patience was tried to the breaking point time after time. There was a Deluge and the purging of the sons of God. That was love. There was Babel and the confusion of tongues. That, too, was love. There was Sodom and Gomorrha — cities not even a haggling Abraham could save. But that brimstone and fire was love. God was ever calling His beloved ones back to Himself. There was Isaac and Jacob, and Jacob's twelve sons. There came Moses, and Aaron, and Josue. Love on God's part; but on man's — there was always sin. God had to be a Lover with infinite patience to put up with this stiff-necked people. He was.

Then came Christ to "an adulterous generation" — only to be done to death. This indeed was love; for he would "cancel the bond with its decrees that was against us . . . by nailing it to the cross" (Col 2:14,15). Christ came with a new mode of love; loving us to death "even to death on a cross," that He might thus love us to life — even to His own Divine Life! "The Law with its commandments and decrees he abolished through his human nature . . . so making peace and reconciling [us] in one body to God by the cross" (Eph 2:14 sqq.).

Before Christ and His Cross, God could love man, but only as His creatures who had some natural participation in His own perfections. But that did not satisfy God. He wanted to love man as His sons, something He could not do so long as they remained unredeemed, so long as they wandered in that "far-off country" of the prodigal son. But after Christ and His Cross, God had His Heart's desire; for "by the blood of Christ those who were far off were brought near" (Eph 2:13). Now God could love man as He had longed to love him since Adam and Eve had forced Him to send the human race into exile. Now He could love man as His son; for the only-Begotten Son had died, risen, ascended, been enthroned, and with the Father had sent the Holy Spirit to vivify men with the life of God. God could now love the children of men not only as His own Child, but as His very spouse! More, He could and would, and now does love man as He loves Himself; for the property of fire is to transform what it touches into itself. The Holy Spirit fell as flame — He fell on you and me and every person baptized.

Paul has described the three periods, the three modes of love, the three manifestations of God thus: "when the designated period of time had elapsed, God sent his Son, born of a woman, born in subjection to the Law, in order to redeem those who were in subjection to the Law, that we might receive the adoption. And because you are sons, God sent the Spirit of his Son into your hearts, crying, 'Abba, Father.' You are, then, no longer a slave but a son; and if a son, an heir also through God's grace" (Gal 4:4–7).

Three periods. Three Persons. Three processes. The Father, in the first period, prepared His people for the coming of His Son by pact, prophets, promises. The Son came. The second period was on; the prophesies were fulfilled, the Law brought to perfection — and men brought closer and closer to God. Finally the third period, that dominated by the Third Person, began at Pentecost, and goes on now. Men have been made sons. Men have been made gods.

"Send forth thy Spirit and they shall be created; and thou shalt renew the face of the earth" (Ps 103:30). You and I sing this psalm frequently in the Liturgy. We have been singing it in our hearts, and by our lives, since we were first conscious of our being. For with that consciousness came a craving to be bigger and better beings than we found ourselves to be. It is our "gravitational pull" toward God. No man can be satisfied with being just a man. The abyss of our next-to-nothingness calls out to the Abyss that is All — God. That craving can be satisfied, thanks to the Fire that fell at Pentecost — and burns in our world today. That Fire sets you aflame with life, with light, with love; for you were baptized with this Fire who is God the Holy Spirit.

Pius XII reminded the world of this truth in his *Mystici*

*Corporis.* "Christ brings the Church to live His own supernatural life," he wrote. "If we examine closely this principle of divine life, we see that it is nothing else than the Holy Spirit, the Paraclete who proceeds from the Father and the Son, and who is called in a special way the 'Spirit of Christ' or the 'Spirit of the Son.' . . . This Spirit Christ merited for us on the Cross. This Spirit He bestowed on the Church . . . so that she and her single members may become daily more and more like our Saviour. . . . This presence and activity of the Spirit of Jesus is tersely and vigorously described by our Predecessor of immortal memory, Leo XIII . . . in these words: 'Let it suffice to say that, as Christ is the Head of the Church, so is the Holy Spirit her soul.' . . . The Church, then, no less than each of her holy members, can make this thought of the Apostle her own: 'And I live, now not I, but Christ lives in me.' . . ." (#69).

It is the soul that unifies all the parts of your body, integrates them into a single whole. The Holy Spirit is the soul of the Mystical Body with similar functions and the same effects. Pius XII continues in the same passage: "To this Spirit of Christ, as to an invisible principle, is to be ascribed the fact that all parts of the body are joined one with the other, and all with their exalted Head; for He [the Holy Spirit] is entire in the Head, entire in the Body, entire in each of the members." The Holy Spirit, then, makes you one with Christ, and Christ makes you one with the Father. If you are "in Christ Jesus," then, you are burning with the very Fire of Holiness. You are one with the Trinity.

In spite of these realities, which none of us can deny, we feel much more like a "limb of Satan" than we do like a branch on Him who is the Vine. The explanation of that paradox you have seen in its source throughout these pages — you are related to Cain as well as to Christ. But you can say with St. Paul: "Well do I know that in me, that is in my lower nature, no good dwells, because to wish is within my power, but I do not find the strength to accomplish what is good. Yes, I do not do the good that I wish, but the evil that I do not wish, that I do. . . . My inner self agrees joyfully with the Law of God, but I see another law in my bodily members warring against the Law which my mind approves. . . . Unhappy man that I am! Who will rescue me. . . . Thanks be to God! [the rescue is effected] through Jesus Christ our Lord" (Rom 7:18–22).

The "new man" has been born. But the "old man" never dies. Hence, we have a work to do. We have to blow the Flame of God, as it were, to ever higher flaming within us so that, in our own degree, we will become what Christ was in supreme degree: "The splendour of the Father's glory." It will require a lifelong effort.

"Tension" is a word today, which too frequently is used to denote abnormality. But that is a mistake, for if you do not feel some tension, know that you are as good as dead. Know, further, that the Spirit of Christ has gone from within you. For, as Christ remarked to His Apostles that last night of His on earth: "If you were children of this world, the world would cherish its own flesh and blood. But you are not children of the world; on the contrary, I have singled you out from the world, and therefore the world hates you" (Jn 15:19). Expect tension from without as well as from within. It is the law of life — especially of life "in Christ Jesus."

There would indeed be an insoluble mystery in your life if you lived as a Christian yet felt no cross. For so long as the Fire of the Holy Spirit burns within you, you will feel your whole being drawn upward, as flame is drawn up. Your being will yearn up toward the Author of being. But at the same time, unlike flame, you will feel a pull earthward. Creatures will draw you downward, even as the Creator draws you upward. Those opposing pulls will make the cross which Christ told you to take up daily. Hence, the feeling of tension from within and from without is evidence that the Living Flame of Love, called the Holy Spirit, is working within you to make you all that God the Father created you to be, and all that God the Son re-created you to be — the Light of the World.

That title recalls the magnificent symbolism seen in the Liturgy of the Paschal Vigil. The unlighted Easter Candle, symbol of the Corpse of Christ, is carried into the dark outside the Church, and the fire, which had been "created" by being struck from a flint, is touched to the candle's wick, and the symbolized Body of Christ becomes alive with light. The glorified Christ is in our midst symbolically. During the next forty days that candle will be quickened into life many times during services. The thoughtful will be reminded of the many comings and goings of the glorified Christ between His Resurrection and Ascension. On Ascension Thursday that candle will not only be extinguished, it will be carried away out of sight. Those sensitive to symbolism will see in the tiny wisp of smoke that rises from the snuffing of the candle, the cloud that received Jesus and took Him from the sight of the Disciples that first Ascension Thursday. The dogmatically sensitive will hear in the voice of the Liturgy the Voice of Christ saying: "It is expedient for you that I go; for if I go I will send the Paraclete . . ." and will be aware once again of the unity of the redemptive act which, beginning at the Annunciation, went on rising in power and luminosity, to be climaxed at Pentecost with the Descent of the Holy Spirit.

That same Flame fell on you — not only at Baptism, but again at Confirmation. He fell on you for the same purpose He fell on the Apostles and disciples the first Pentecost: to transform you. He fell on you to make you *Lumen Christi* — and thus become the "Light of the World."

In the first sermon Jesus Christ gave, according to St. Matthew's Gospel, the truth we are trying to bring home to you was told by Truth Himself. To his hearers that day of the Sermon on the Mount, and through them to you and me, Christ said: "You are the light of the world . . . so let your light shine before your fellowmen, that they may see your good example, and praise your Father who is in Heaven" (Mt 5:14–16).

Love tells the whole story. Creation is attributed to the love of the Father; Re-creation, to the love of the Son; Sanctification, which spells salvation, to the love of the Holy Spirit. It is in this last work that you are engaged. You are to love with the very love of God, and you can do it; for "God's love is poured forth into our hearts by the Holy Spirit who has been given to us" (Rom 5:5).

Love is the key to every mystery in the life of Christ and to every mystery in the life of every true Christian. It laughs at

definition, but it has been described. The life of Christ is one
long description of what love is, and what love does. He also
gave us a description in words: "If you love . . . keep the commandments." And again: "Greater love than this no man has . . .,"
and even more pertinently: "A new commandment I give you:
love one another." If that be too general, too vague, then turn
to Paul's Hymn to Love as found in that famed thirteenth chapter
of his First to the Corinthians. There he specifies and tells you that
love is "long suffering, kind, not envious, not given to bragging,
not conceited, ill-mannered, selfseeking, irritable. . . . That it is
always ready to make allowances, to trust, to hope, to be patient. . . ." That was Jesus Christ. That must be every true
Christian.

Conscious of our many failings, we often quail at Paul's description of love, which we know is our life's calling. But that is the
time to recall with Romano Guardini: "The believer does well
to say, not that he is a Christian, but that he is trying to become
one." That, precisely, is your life's work and mine. We must be
patient with ourselves, even as we are importunate with God. We
can plague Him with our pleas. Our hearts should be naught but
a steady pulsing plea of: *Veni, Sancte Spiritus* — "Come, Holy
Spirit!"

God will hear, and you can walk the world's noisy streets
aglow with God.

But before we can claim to have solved the mysteries in your
life fully, we must look and find the Woman in your life. Christ's
Spirit will lead us to her; for He is her Spouse. . . .

# CHAPTER SIXTEEN

# The Mystery Woman in Your Life

~~~~~~~~~~~~~~~~~~~~~~~~~~~~~~~~~~~~~~~~~~~

*"Woman, behold . . ."*

THERE is a woman in every man's life — most always, there are many women, not in the current sense of sex and sensuality, but in the sense God had in His mind when He fashioned woman from the side of man and made her to be man's helpmate. And to a degree, sometimes unsuspected, the solution to most of the mysteries in any man's life lies with the woman God gave each individual to be his mother. For it is through her that God has willed to transmit many of those characteristics which will set the individual off from the rest of mankind.

This study opened with the two women who have had most to do with you and your life. You met them again and again as you unraveled the skein of your mysterious life. Now if you will look more closely you will see that it is *you* they hold in their arms. They are your mothers. From each you inherited much. From Eve, your mother according to the flesh, you inherited many of your physical, and even many of your psychic qualities and characteristics. But from the other woman you have received those qualities and characteristics that can make you all God means you to be. For Mary is your Mother according to that inheritance that came to you from Him who died on the Cross; she is also Mediatrix of all grace. And, as you have learned again and again in these pages, grace is your real life; for it is a share in the life of God.

It is true that there were many women in Christ's life; and it is highly rewarding to study Christ's attitudes and relations toward each of them. But here all we will do is make the suggestion then

189

point to one striking fact. As we think of Christ's public life we are prone to picture Him trudging the dusty roads of Palestine with only the Twelve near Him and the rest of the disciples — all men — coming behind. But there is a passage at the close of St. Luke's narration of Calvary's events which tells about "the women who had accompanied him from Galilee" (23:55). It was they who accompanied Him to Calvary and "stood by, watching what was going on." They were faithful when all the men who had accompanied Him through life had fled. They were faithful to the end — even to the burial. Manifesting what is best in womanhood, they showed themselves utterly forgetful of self, totally immersed in thought of the beloved. Just as they, to the shame of all the men who loved Him, were the last to leave Calvary and the tomb on Friday, so were they the first to hurry toward the tomb on Easter Sunday morning. Small wonder that the Christ in glory showed Himself first to these women!

But *the* woman of His life was "the woman above all women blest" — His Mother. She was the woman not only of His life, but also of His Death — His Resurrection, Ascension, and Enthronement; she was the woman of Pentecost; she is the woman of His life in glory. For, since God is just, His balance is always perfect. As Mary shared in Christ's sufferings, sorrows, and disgrace, so, in proper proportion, she now shares in Christ's glory. But just as He is ever active on your behalf in that Kingdom beyond time, so is she — this Queen of the Universe, who is your Mother by God's decree and Christ's "last will and testament." Hence, if you will live as God and the God-Man would have you live, *the* woman in your life will be Mary.

The first "Annunciation" came directly from the lips of God the Creator at the time He found His first two human creatures ashamed, as it were, of their flesh because they had sinned. At that moment — one of the highest in human history — God promised that His Son would take flesh, and by suffering in that flesh, redeem all flesh. That first of all "annunciations" was made to your mother according to the flesh — Eve. The second Annunciation was made to your Mother according to the Spirit — Mary. But even that record does not complete the "annunciations" that mark the mysteries in your life. There was a third, and a very important and personal one, made on Calvary's top when the dying Christ, "seeing his mother and the disciple whom he loved standing by, said to his mother: 'Mother, this is your son.'" (Jn 19:26.) That was the "annunciation" that Mary was to be the Mother of the Mystical Body; for though Jesus spoke directly about and to St. John, He spoke to him not so much as an individual, but as representative of all humankind. Mary was made Mother then just as really as she had been made Mother at Nazareth. And just as nine months had to elapse between that Annunciation and the appearance of "the blessed fruit of her womb," so more than fifty days had to pass between this "annunciation" and the day the world would look upon the Mystical Body of Christ in the persons of the Apostles and those disciples who had "with one mind continued steadfastly in prayer with some women and Mary, the Mother of Jesus" (Acts 1:14).

The "annunciation" on Calvary was followed in Jerusalem, just as the Annunciation in Nazareth had been followed, by the "overshadowing of the Holy Spirit." It is stimulating when reciting the Creed to see the similarity between the physical Christ and the mystical Christ. We say we believe "in Jesus Christ . . . who was conceived by the Holy Spirit . . . born of the Virgin Mary." The Spirit and the Bride gave Christ to the world in that flesh with which He redeemed the world. And it is the Spirit and the Bride who gave the world the Mystical Christ so that the world that has been redeemed may yet be saved. True it is that the Mystical Body of Christ was born from the side of Christ on Calvary, as Pius XII says in his *Mystici Corporis,* but the "Epiphany" of that Christ came only after the Spirit had fallen as Flame on Pentecost. So, since Mary was there, we can say that the Spirit and the Bride gave the world the Mystical Jesus — and never forget that it is the Spirit and the Bride who give the individual soul the Christ-life.

A decade has passed since the Marian Year — 1954. In that year one heard again and again that we were living in the "Age of Mary." Pius XII did all he could to focus attention on "this woman above all women blest." It was he who gave us the official pronouncement which made her Assumption an article of Faith. He it was who gave us that feast which proclaims her Queen of the Universe. And it was he who taught what Pius X had already taught, and what each of us Christians should never have any need to be taught; namely, that the Mother of Christ is the Mother of every Christian; the Mother of the physical Jesus is Mother of His Mystical Body; that just as she carried Him in her womb physically, so she carried each of us there spiritually.

In the words of theologian Father Paul Segneri: "The life of man is nothing else than a continual liberality of Mary." That is a simple statement of God's plan in and for your life. If Mary be the Gateway of grace, and if grace be nothing other than a share in God's life, you can see that Mary is the Gateway of life.

It has been profoundly gratifying to watch the growth of the theology on Mary this past half century. Our theologians have found the basic principle of Mariology to be the immutable, salvific Will of God. She is the woman in your life simply because God willed her to be. That is why this book opens and closes with Mary — as *Madonna,* your Mother! — and as *Pietá,* the tender Mother who will receive you into her arms at death. It is Mary who shows us that God's plan is all of a piece; for just as she played a major part in all the mysteries of Christ's life, so she plays the same part in the mysteries of your life. As St. Bernard, echoing St. Augustine, once wrote: "One man and one woman harmed us grievously. Thanks be to God all things are restored by one Man and one Woman — and that with interest. It is true that Christ would have been adequate, since all our sufficiency is from Him. But it was not good for us that it should be by a Man alone. It was more appropriate that both sexes should take part in our reparation, since both had wrought our ruin" (*Serm 1 de 12 Praerog.*).

This study has been a practical attempt to show how you can live the mystery-filled life that is yours with clarity of mind, a focused will, and a God-consciousness that gives you continual joy. Throughout the ages, and very pointedly throughout this present age, God bas-reliefs the truth the times need to see. In the middle of our sex-preoccupied century He had His Vicar proclaim the dogma which tells the present glory of Mary's flesh, foretells the future glory of our own flesh, and alerts us to the glorious duty of the day which we are to discharge in and through the flesh.

To speak of the "body beautiful" is to use current language which has no religious connotation. Yet the theological fact is that the climaxing act of Creation came when God fashioned the human body, and He made that body beautiful. From the beautiful body of Mary Immaculate there came forth the Body of the "most beautiful of the sons of men." Those two glorified bodies are now in Heaven and are promises concerning your own body. And those two beautiful bodies, which were instrumental in your Redemption, are now being instrumental in your salvation.

Since "there is no lovelier way to thank God for your sight than by giving a helping hand to those in the dark"; and since this Age of the Mystical Body, this Marian Age, is also an Age of Sex and Sin, we shall look upon this Woman in your life and learn from her the sacredness of human flesh, the sublime grandeur of motherhood, the holiness of virginity.

Our present century has employed everything within its power to call attention to the fact that the human body is appealing and can yet be made more appealing. This glorification of human flesh has become a cult – a pagan cult, of course. In our day the word "flesh" has come to hold connotations that it should never be permitted. We think too readily of sins of the flesh, when our Christian minds should ever and always associate sacredness with that word. For three times a day many a Catholic will pause to recite the *Angelus* — prayerfully commemorating the greatest event of all history. In that prayer the apex of the mystery is recalled as we say: "And the Word was made *flesh*." It is the all-holy God we speak of when we say "The Word." We are telling the most magnificent manifestation of His all-holy love for us when we say "was made flesh." We are also adumbrating the full sweep of those mysteries of Christ that mean everything to man — and almost as much to God. It was in the flesh and through the flesh that infinite reparation was made to God because of sin. It is through the flesh and in the flesh that eternal salvation comes to man. Because formerly every Mass, practically speaking, ended with the words "And the Word was made *flesh*," no one should now hear the word without hearing something of the infinite holiness of God and the sacredness of all human flesh.

Our contemporaries need to think theologically about their own flesh; for when anyone thinks rightly about being "in Christ Jesus" he has to think through to a veritable theology of the flesh. Once you do that, you see what a place Mary has in your life, and that this Woman of all women is truly the Queen of Theology.

Many of us, if not most of us, would be inclined to think Mary's influence on the theology of the Church began at the Council at Ephesus in the year 431, when Nestorius, the then Bishop of Constantinople, was condemned for teaching that Mary was mother only of the Man Jesus, and not Mother of God. It was in that council that the word *Theotokos* "God-bearer," was used of Mary. But centuries before that, Mary had exerted powerful influence on theological thought. How could it be otherwise when she was Mother of the mystical Christ as well as the physical Jesus? She had to mother the infant Church just as she had mothered the Infant Christ. She had to teach the Apostles much the same as she had taught Jesus — and that she did from His Ascension to her own Assumption. St. Luke's Gospel bears implicit testimony to this; for this doctor-evangelist gives us fact after fact that could have been learned only from Mary. And Mary's influence on this theology of the flesh today is just as implicit. When our Pragmatist, God, has His Vicar, Pius XII, promulgate the dogma of Mary's Assumption and proclaim the Feast of her Universal Queenship, He was again showing how true it is to say of Mary: "Alone thou hast stamped out all heresies."

One of the earliest heresies in the Church was that of the *Docetists*. These men simply could not believe that God would take flesh. They said He only "seemed" to. In Greek the word *dokein* means "to make believe." So these men are called Docetists; for their doctrine is a doctrine about God's playing "make-believe." They said the Word only "appeared" to take flesh; He did not do so in reality. Hence, He only "seemed" to suffer and die in the flesh. Basically their error stemmed from an attitude toward the flesh that seems as old as man, best known as "Manichaean," which is based on a concept that flesh is evil by its very nature.

Five hundred years before Mary said *"Fiat"* so that God could take flesh in and from her flesh, Zoroaster in Persia and Buddha in India were teaching in their own ways the error that seems never to die; they were inculcating in their disciples an antagonism to the flesh that God had made and "saw that it was good." Christianity had hardly been born (in and through the Flesh of Christ) when Gnostics and Docetists were teaching the same fundamental error.

It does one's heart good to hear that grand old man, Ignatius of Antioch, in the year 107 thundering against these heretics: "Stop your ears when anyone speaks to you who stands apart from Jesus Christ, David's Scion and Mary's Son, who was actually born, who actually ate and drank, who actually suffered under Pontius Pilate, who was actually crucified and who actually died while heaven and earth and the underworld looked on; who also actually rose from the dead, since His Father raised Him up — His Father who will likewise raise up all who believe in Him through Jesus Christ, apart from whom we have no real life."*

What a theology of the flesh one could enucleate from that brave passage. How like our own Apostle's Creed it sounds! Ignatius stressed the truth that it is the Flesh of Christ that redeemed us and even gave promise of an eternity for us in a flesh glorified as His own is — flesh that will know agility, subtlety, impassibility, and immortality like that known by the flesh of Mary Immaculate and the Flesh of her firstborn Son. But to stress the Flesh of Jesus is implicitly, at least, to lay heavy stress on the flesh of Mary, His Mother. Hence, from Ignatius' words a theologian could show how all the privileges and prerogatives that make Mary so surpassingly peerless really depend on and derive, in a way, from her flesh. Because she was to mother the Christ she had been conceived in the flesh immaculately. In her flesh she was virgin before she conceived by the Holy Spirit, virgin at the birth of her Son, and remained a virgin ever after. And because that Immaculate Heart of hers, which was to be run through by those Seven Swords of Sorrow, was a heart of flesh, it is evident that in the flesh and through the flesh she can be called Coredemptrix. In that same flesh,

---

* *Mary and Modern Man* (America Press, 1954), p. 112.

in which she stood beneath the Cross of Christ, she was assumed into Heaven, and there crowned Queen of the universe. In that flesh she reigns today and because she is Gateway of all grace, is really our Gateway to Heaven.

With those facts about human flesh before us, does it not seem most strange to find those ancient Persians, Greeks, and Indians, followed by the Gnostics in the first three centuries of the Christian era, the Manichaeans in the fourth and fifth, Albigensians and Catharists in the twelfth and thirteenth, Illuminati, Quietists, and others in the sixteenth and seventeenth — and now on into our own twentieth century — either despising the flesh or indulging it?

Of course no one needs to be told that heresy lies also in the opposite extreme to this one which looks upon flesh as evil. Today, too many look upon it as so good in itself that it needs no discipline, no control, no denial of its often imperious demands. Flesh is sacred because it is animated by a spiritual, immortal soul. Flesh is sacred because it is destined for an eternity with the soul that animated it during earthly existence. One might dare say that our human flesh is sacred because of the sacredness of Mary and the Son she bore — she is "our tainted nature's solitary boast." The nature the rest of us have *is* tainted — and since that nature functions in and through the flesh we will not exaggerate in either way: flesh is not to be despised as evil, nor is it to be indulged as the only good! It is to be respected, reverenced, and considered holy because it is God's choice of envelope for that soul which bears His image and likeness, because He so loved men who lived in the flesh that He assumed it and through it redeemed men, and because He has destined the flesh of man to be where Mary's is now — provided men use it after the fashion Mary used hers.

Do we not make implicit profession of our determination to do just that: to use our flesh as Mary used hers — every time we recite that common prayer of Christians — the Hail Mary? In the first half, which is truly the "Angelical Salutation," since it repeats the words of Gabriel, we really "anathematize" every heretic who looks upon the flesh as evil when we proclaim that the "fruit of her womb" is "blessed." When we hail her as "full of grace" and salute her for having "the Lord with her," we condemn the materialist and hedonist.

This familiar prayer, brief though it be, is so replete with revealed truths about God and ourselves, that the subtlest minds of all past centuries have not exhausted it — even as the simplest minds of every century will always understand it. It is also resonant with much human and divine history. It recalls to the well-read those victories at Muret, Lepanto, and Vienna — where civilizations were saved in the thirteenth, sixteenth, and late seventeenth centuries. But to the theologically-minded it is filled with the sound of God's own voice when He made the first "annunciation" in Eden, and with the Voice of God's own Word as He made that final "annunciation" on Calvary. From this perfect prayer one can uncover not only Mariology but all Christology as well. It holds in its depths a very clear Christian anthropology too. And that is why it should be beating in our hearts at all times as we move through this life on toward that other where a share in His and her triple triumph awaits us — in the flesh!

Pius XII made all this quite explicit in *Munificentissimus Deus,* in which he defined the dogma of Mary's Assumption. After giving the reason for defining the dogma at this particular moment in history as being to "the advantage of human society," the Pope turned toward the children of the Roman Catholic Church and told them he was defining this glory of Mary so that "all the faithful will be stirred to a stronger piety toward their heavenly Mother." "Stronger piety" means anything but "pietism." It means devotedness, commitment, dedication. It means deliberate, whole-souled obedience to Mary and her maternal commands and requests. She has made many this past century — as Lourdes, La Salette, Pontmain, Fatima, Beauraing, and Banneux, to name a few of the places she has appeared — and always with the same message: "Pray and do penance." That means use of the flesh for God's glory and the salvation of men. The Pope then directed his attention to those Christians not in the Catholic Church and told them he was defining Mary's Assumption with them in mind, too, hoping "that all those who glory in the Christian name may be moved by the desire of sharing in the unity of Jesus Christ's Mystical Body and of increasing their love for her who shows her heart to all the members of this august Body."

But the Pope would not be the Vicar of Christ if he did not have all men in mind whenever he spoke officially, or prayed personally. Hence, it is not surprising to have Pius XII reveal that he had his hand on the pulse of the world, knew just how its heart was beating, and could even hazard a definite prognosis about its functioning tomorrow. Mary is close to that beating heart. That is why Pius dared to say: "Thus, [by pointing to Mary and her glorious Assumption] while the illusory teachings of materialism and the corruption of morals that follows from these teachings threaten to extinguish the light of virtue and to ruin the lives of men by exciting discord among them, in this magnificent way all may see clearly to what a lofty goal our bodies are destined."

Men today need to know that goal; for, while destruction of the body is ever threatened from without, and an actual slow dissolution of it goes on from within, man must know that he is destined for more than destruction or dissolution. That is why Pius closed his list of reasons for his Definition with the words: "Finally, it is our hope that belief in Mary's bodily assumption into heaven will make our belief in our own resurrection stronger and render it more effective" (#42).

When we say our Hail Mary now, and come to that last petition in which we plead with her to "pray for us sinners now and at the hour of our death," let us realize we are identifying ourselves with Cain and with Christ; that we would live as her children and die as her Son died; that we would have her mother us throughout life and receive us into her arms at death, so that she could take us into that Kingdom where He reigns as King and she is Queen-Mother.

That simple prayer offers the solution to our mystery-filled lives; for it shows us the unity in all our dogmas, the magnificent clarity to God's plan, the interrelation of all the mysteries in Christ's life and in Mary's living.

Just as her Assumption and Coronation were contained in her Immaculate Conception, so is our final resurrection and eternal life with God contained in our Baptism. But just as she had to go through the events which are the fourteen mysteries we commemorate on our Rosaries before she could pass through the nine choirs of angels up to that seat beside the throne of her Son, so shall we have to live the Joyful and the Sorrowful Mysteries before we will know the fullness and the finality in the last of the Glorious ones.

The same Paul who has taught us so much about the mysteries in our lives is the one who tells us about our own coronation in Heaven. Mary had hers because she was the Mother of Christ. We will have ours if we live as His members. For just as we can say with Paul: "Christ is my life," so long as we move through our mysteries, so we will be able to say, as we near the end, what he said to Timothy: "I have fought the good fight, I have finished the course, I have kept the faith. What remains is the crown . . ." (2 Tm 4:8). On Paul's own word that crown awaits us provided we do as he did; for it is "the crown due to holiness which the Lord, the just Judge, will give to those who love his brilliant coming."

If we would fight that good fight, finish that course Paul tells about, and keep the faith, we will do well to hear Mary calling to us as only a mother could call: "I am the Mother of Fair Love . . . and of Holy Hope. . . . In me is all Grace of the Way . . . in me is all Hope of Life. . . . Come over to me, all you that desire me; and be filled with my fruits" (Ecclus 24:24–26).

The child in every human being should answer that call; and the man, hearing her calling, "might rise and thunder on the doors of the grave."

We found the first woman in your life as a bereaved sinner — outside Paradise. We find *the* Woman of your life — enthroned in Heaven, living there as does her Son, present at the Eternal Sacrifice of her Son, for the same purpose she was present on Calvary: to be Christ's Mother who with Him would coredeem all Christ's members. By that eternal decree, which we have seen so often dominating the mysteries of our life, the Mother of God is also our Mother. St. Proclus had reason to call Mary "the only bridge of God to men." So did St. Bernard have divinely deep reason to say: "We have everything through Mary." That reason was the decree mentioned above, which is God's Will articulated, that we return to Paradise where our mystery-filled lives are supposed to end — only to begin an eternal mystery of life and love with the Eternal Mystery who is God.